'A joy! Michael and Pippa have created something truly magical and meaningful. A book of delicious surprises that dances between precision, technique and artisanship – as well as old school values, represented by flavours picked from the seasons of our lives. A special book from a special team, Michael and Pippa live and breathe these recipes, and it shows from the first page to the last.'

Darren Purchese

—

'From inspiring flavours to informed methods, gorgeous photos and bushels of compelling recipes, Michael and Pippa James show us how to save, cherish and celebrate the bounty of all seasons. I cannot wait to bake my way from short affairs (wholemeal shortbreads) to mini projects (cardamom palmiers!) and beyond. This book – a deep reference, chock-full of learnings, guidance and deliciousness – offers more than one-off bakes, it inspires us to live more. To bake more. And to share the sweetness of all seasons with those around us.'

Martin Philip

Sweet Seasons

Wholesome treats
for every occasion

Michael and
Pippa James

Sweet
Seasons

Wholesome treats
for every occasion

Hardie Grant

BOOKS

For Tina and Geoff.

Contents

Word came to me quickly on the bakers' grapevine when Michael and Pippa James opened the Tivoli Road Bakery, the shop they ran in Melbourne for six years. People kept telling me about this fantastic new bakery that had set up in an unlikely side street in South Yarra. Being naturally greedy and requiring little in the way of encouragement when it comes to exploring new bakeries, I made a beeline for it the next time I was in Melbourne.

It was totally my kind of place. The cakes were honest, unassuming and delicious. More than a bakery, it was the type of place that somehow becomes the centre of a kind of community. You could feel it from the vibe the minute you walked in. Being someone who frequented the Tivoli Road Bakery was something that became part of your identity, that created immediate common ground when someone else told you they went there as well. I went whenever I was in Melbourne and needed something delightful to take to a friend. Or when I just needed something delightful, period.

In their first book, *The Tivoli Road Baker*, Michael and Pippa let us in on some of the secrets that made their bakery such a much-loved gem. Now, two books later, in *Sweet Seasons*, they give us something even more personal.

There are stories here of a Cornish childhood and ingredients plucked from fruit trees in a Canberra garden, a great-aunt's treasured recipe and cakes remembered from a family cafe in times long gone. Michael and Pippa show us that a bake isn't just a combination of ingredients melded by heat, but something that reaches into other people's lives, across space, across time, and is in turn, carried forward to reach ever further.

How true that is! For us bakers (and if you're reading this, you're probably one of us), baking isn't some unavoidable chore thrown up by the grind of life, like taking out the bins. It's a way we find self-expression, nurture our relationships, celebrate or stand with our community. It's a way we restore ourselves and heal others. That current of connection runs through this book.

But *Sweet Seasons* isn't just an ode to the different ways of marking the year with baking. There are recipes here that you'll use when you have time to immerse yourself deeply in the magic of baking, and others you'll use when you only have twenty minutes to produce something that will bring a smile to someone's face. If you're a newcomer to our tribe (Welcome!), there are foundational recipes that will induct you into the art and give you the confidence to go further. And recognising the realities of our over-consumerised lives, Michael and Pippa show us how we can create a more sustainable (and flavourful) way of baking, using wholegrain flours and alternatives to refined sugars.

Sweet Seasons isn't just another one for the bookshelf. This is one to cherish.

Helen Goh
London

Sweet Seasons is offered as a reference for sweet baking throughout the year, and also over the years. The recipes emulate the rhythms and seasons of our lives, from annual gluts to family celebrations and festive gatherings. We are also reflecting on the role food has played in our lives at different times, sometimes nourishing the soul with a little comfort, at other times offering quick sustenance or something fun to bake with our daughter. The food that we eat has enormous significance on our quality of life, as individuals and in our community.

Our food stories are different. Michael grew up in Cornwall, with a grandmother who baked Cornish classics for afternoon tea following weekend sports activities. He went on to become a chef and then a highly skilled baker. He holds a vast repertoire of recipes developed in restaurants and bakeries, but he is also tethered to the place of his birth when he makes saffron buns, heavy cake and ginger fairings. These beautiful bakes speak of the history and landscapes of Cornwall, creating a visceral experience in the eating.

Pippa grew up in Canberra, with an abundant veggie garden and a few fruit trees. The Burley Griffin vision of quarter-acre blocks providing small-scale self-reliance was embedded into her childhood – homegrown, homemade tomato sauce was traded, recipes for preserving gluts were exchanged, dishes were shared with a spirit of generosity. She learned that food is a great connector – to the seasons, the land, and to others. Pippa's mother was an excellent baker and opened one of Canberra's first cafes, offering exquisite cakes, slices and more. She cooked with whole food and a whole lot of love – freshly ground nuts and wholemeal flour were staples. At the height of production she was baking 60 cakes a day, many of them at home, and we're thrilled to share some of her indelible repertoire here, albeit with some updates.

Together, one of our long-favoured pastimes is indulging in new recipes and techniques over a weekend. We might see what's in the garden and then visit a farmers' market seeking the season's bounty. We'll deliberate what to cook over morning tea, before spending an entire afternoon preparing and cooking a feast for people we love. This kind of gathering and generous sharing offers space to slow down and rejuvenate body and soul, providing a sort of spiritual sustenance that sometimes feels like it belongs in the past. We can meaningfully connect to people, place, seasons and ourselves through our food rituals.

It's idyllic, but in all honesty, those weekends are rare in this particular season of our lives. With a young child and the competing demands of a busy family schedule, there is (much!) less time to prepare food and less creative brain-space to think about it. But we still want to eat delicious and nourishing food, and over the years we've honed our skills and knowledge so that we can eat while staying true to our ethics, even in a hurry.

These days we also love to include our daughter in the kitchen. She's always loved to measure, mix and taste. Cooking improves kids' dexterity, maths skills, creativity and openness to trying new flavours. It's also just fun to get messy and see what they come up with, and it teaches them what real food is.

In railing against the refined sugars hidden in so much of what's offered as food on supermarket shelves, we find ourselves exploring different ways to sweeten things up. We use less white sugar and more honey or unrefined cane sugars. Of course, they all have their place, but more and more we find that a greater depth of flavour, robust texture and the absence of a sugar rush bring more pleasure.

So, here we offer simple recipes for satisfying weekday fixes, slow immersions to remind you that baking can also be therapy and – hopefully – give you the confidence to master the foundations and create your own dishes with what you have to hand. We wholeheartedly believe that the way we choose to eat creates a ripple from your centre to your loved ones, your community and ultimately across the globe. You get to choose the impact you'll have.

Choose wisely. Stay sweet.

If you truly cook seasonally, you will find yourself reaching for trusty base recipes that can be adapted according to the produce available. *Seasons harnessed* offers reliable pastry recipes to form the foundations of your repertoire and give you the confidence to create your own recipes. The *Seasons altered* notes throughout the book offer tips for adaptation and inspiration. This is the most satisfying way to cook, building confidence in technique and flavour combinations.

Seasons past is our little indulgence, filled with recipes from our childhoods, from Cornish favourites to Brown poles (yes, it's a thing!). *Seasons fast* contains the recipes we reach for when time is tight and we need something delicious and comforting. *Seasons savoured* is a reminder that baking can be an exercise in self-soothing, and of the reward in spending time making something beautiful. Yes, baking can be frustrating and intimidating, but if you let go of perfection and take the time to enjoy it, baking can also be a therapeutic pastime.

Seasons shared holds the keys to feeding others. These are recipes that travel well, either as individual pieces or large-format bakes to slice and share. We've also snuck in some of our dinner party favourites. *Seasons marked* offers recipes for highlights of the calendar year, from hot cross buns at Easter to stone fruit galettes at the height of summer. Finally, *Seasons captured* shows how we take produce at its peak and bottle it for future enjoyment.

There is a note below on some techniques, and step-by-step instructions with images are scattered through the book.

We write with the intention to inspire rather than to purely instruct. Once you understand the basics, you can start to tinker and adapt. Rather than spending time traipsing after specific ingredients, use what you have and see where it takes you. There is creative freedom in starting with less. Just as boredom sparks imagination, having limited ingredients can inspire new combinations that become fast favourites.

Over the following pages is a non-exhaustive range of advice on equipment, measurements, ingredients and techniques to support you on your journey.

Equipment

You can do a lot without a full set of gadgets and gizmos, just as our grandparents did. Your hands are the ultimate baking tool, and nothing beats getting them into the mix. But a good food processor and a stand mixer will save you time and effort, and often result in a better bake – more aeration in the mixing equals light and fluffy deliciousness. Experience has taught us that cheap equipment (just like cheap food) usually has a hidden cost, and that investing in better machinery and taking care of it can save you money in the long run.

Use a traditional 'roller' style rolling pin for rolling pastry – one with handles at each end, attached to a central dowel that it rolls around. This requires less effort, from both you and the dough. Our large straight rolling pin is great for softening butter-rich doughs. We have invested in nice wooden rolling pins that are a pleasure to use.

Aside from your big kit, a range of inexpensive kitchen items will make your baking time more enjoyable, including:

- dough scraper
- pastry brush
- reusable piping bag, with various nozzles
- offset spatula
- digital scales.

We have a messy drawer full of tins, moulds and cutters in different sizes. These recipes are designed to 'fit' certain tin sizes, but don't feel you need to forgo a recipe or rush out to buy a new tin for the sake of a couple of centimetres. You can simply divide the mixture between two smaller tins, or pour any excess batter into a muffin tin. Just be mindful that you may need to adjust the bake time – a smaller cake will bake more quickly, and so will a flatter one, so set the timer for a shorter bake and keep a close eye on the oven.

All recipes have been tested in a domestic fan-forced oven. If using a conventional oven, increase the temperature by 20°C (70°F). Having said that, each oven has its own unique personality, and oven temperatures and bake times can vary. Hopefully you have gotten to know yours over the years, and can use your baking intuition.

Measurements

Correct measurements are essential to successful baking. This is why bakers prefer to measure ingredients by weight rather than volume, and why it's a good idea to use reliable scales that measure to the gram.

In a domestic kitchen, however, sometimes it's easier to measure smaller amounts by volume. Standard cup and tablespoon measurements vary internationally. Below are the standard measures for Australia, UK and USA.

	Australia	UK	USA
Tablespoon	20 ml (¾ fl oz)	15 ml (½ fl oz)	15 ml (½ fl oz)
Cup	250 ml (8½ fl oz)	284 ml (9½ fl oz)	236 ml (8 fl oz)

Measuring by volume can be less precise so it's worth being meticulous. All volume measures given in this book are based on Australian standard measures.

Ingredients

SOURCING

Modern, global food systems are designed to be convenient and highly profitable for a small number of people. Worldwide, food production is one of the biggest carbon-emitting industries, contributing significantly to the climate crisis and causing immense environmental damage. The shift towards globalised food systems over the last century or so, largely driven by corporate interests, has neatly coincided with an enormous increase in human disease.

In short, our food systems are making us, and our home planet, sick. So the food you buy and where you buy it are important.

Aside from environmental and health factors, ingredients such as sugar and cacao have dark colonial histories, and their industries have had terrible social impacts. We are starting to see more ethical chocolate producers and alternative sugars, which is encouraging. There is much to learn, and much to heal.

But this is a recipe book, not a food systems manifesto, so we'll keep this brief. In general, we think it's a good idea to:

- buy and eat whole foods, and avoid ultra-processed foods

- buy local, seasonal produce and use it all up

- support local farmers and keep your money circulating in your community by shopping at farmers' markets or small greengrocers

- grow some food, even herbs on a window sill

- ask questions, read widely and learn as much as you can about the impact of your food choices.

If this has piqued your curiosity, check the resources listed at the back of the book for further reading.

SUGAR

We love eating sweet stuff, but find many recipes have more sugar than required. In testing for this book, we've generally pared back the sugar and introduced less refined sugar where it works. Following is some information about different sweeteners. It's non-exhaustive, but reflects what we use most in our cooking.

Golden caster sugar, or raw caster sugar, is an unrefined fine sugar that's a great substitute for white caster sugar. We do use **caster (superfine) sugar** as well, and keep it in a large jar with used vanilla beans to infuse.

Rapadura sugar is an unrefined cane sugar made in Central and Latin America. There are similar styles of unrefined sugar from different regions, such as **panela** and **piloncillo**. They have subtle differences, but will perform in a similar way, as will **coconut sugar**. Using unrefined sugar instead of caster sugar can and will change a recipe's texture. Unrefined sugar contains more moisture, which can impact the performance, and the flavour will be bolder and richer.

Soft brown sugar is refined granulated sugar that is re-blended with syrup and treacle to give it its brown colour. **Dark brown sugar** or **muscovado sugar** is a partially refined sugar with more molasses added back in, resulting in a darker colour and deeper flavour.

Demerara sugar is raw sugar extracted from sugarcane. It is minimally processed, and not fine like caster sugar. We use it to finish pastry bakes because the large grains give a rustic appearance, lovely crunch and delightful bursts of sweetness without over-sweetening the dish.

Molasses and **treacle** are a byproduct of the sugar-making process, and have long been used in traditional European breads, pastries and cakes to give the bakes a rich, deep flavour. After the juice is extracted from sugarcane or sugar beets, it is boiled down to form the crystals we know as table sugar. Molasses is the thick, brown syrup left over after they remove the crystals from the juice. Treacle is commonly known as the British version of molasses: thick and dark, sweet and slightly bitter.

Maple syrup is the sap of the maple tree, mostly harvested in North America. In early spring, as the days start to warm but the nights are still cold, the sap liquifies within the tree and a small tap is knocked into the trunk for it to run out of. The very light, slightly sweet liquid is then boiled down for many hours to produce a delicious amber syrup.

We use **honey** in our baking and cooking as a natural way of adding sweetness. Honey is made and stored to nourish bee colonies as well as ourselves, and pure honey holds antibacterial and immune-boosting properties. Buy unadulterated honey from local hives where possible.

FLOUR AND GRAIN

Flours ain't flours. For centuries, all over the world, civilisations have been built and sustained by a huge variety of grains, ground into flour for myriad applications. Today, a far smaller variety is widely available, such as spelt, rye and single variety or population wheats. There are many non-glutinous grain flours as well, which we use for different purposes. These are all worth exploring for the sake of flavour, nutrition and biodiversity. Bear in mind that flour will perform differently depending on the variety, proportion of the wholegrain and freshness. That is a whole other book (we delve more into flours in our first book, *The Tivoli Road Baker*) but here is a quick guide to selecting and substituting flours.

Plain (all-purpose) flour is the most commonly used wheat flour. It has had the bran and germ stripped out during the milling process to increase the shelf life of the flour as well as consistency in baked products. **Wholegrain or wholemeal flour** still contains all of the grain after milling, so it has more available nutrients and dietary fibre. It also has a whole lot more flavour and texture, but it's worth remembering that this will diminish as the flour ages. If you are using wholegrain flour, buy the freshest you can and use it quickly. Even better, buy the grain and mill your own flour.

In general, wholegrain flours will absorb more liquid than plain flour. If you are substituting plain flour for wholegrain, you may need to decrease the flour in the recipe by up to 10 per cent, or add a little more liquid or fat. It's a good idea to try the recipe with plain flour first, so you know the texture you're aiming for.

Bakers (strong) flour contains more protein and is generally used for bread because the stronger gluten bonds hold their structure, resulting in a lovely open crumb. Use this for babka, brioche and hot cross buns. 'Soft', 'plain' or 'cake' flour contains less gluten and results in the soft, tender crumb that you want to achieve in cakes.

Different types of **nut flours** are widely available in supermarkets and bulk food stores. Because of their high fat content, ground nuts oxidise quickly, and for this reason we prefer to grind whole nuts ourselves. Nuts with a very high fat content, like pistachios or macadamias, benefit from being frozen before grinding. The cold stops them getting smooshed in the blades of your food processor and allows you to achieve a finer grind. Just be careful to stop before your nuts turn to butter.

EGGS

When mixing cakes or batters, always use eggs at room temperature. And weigh your eggs. Whether the recipe calls for one egg or ten, crack them into a bowl over a set of scales. Eggs vary in size, and ensuring accuracy will give better results. Most recipes in this book call for medium eggs, 50 g (1¾ oz) once cracked. A medium yolk will be 20 g (¾ oz), the white will be 30 g (1 oz).

Once your eggs are cracked, give them a quick whisk before adding them to your dough so they emulsify more quickly and give better aeration. This applies when adding eggs to pastry dough, batters or bread doughs like babkas, hot cross buns and other similar bun doughs.

Always, always use truly free-range eggs. There are many good eggs available these days, and it's worth seeking the best you can – you will notice the difference in flavour and performance.

DAIRY PRODUCTS

Butter is one of the most important ingredients in baking. Always bake with unsalted butter. Cultured butter is generally more flavoursome, the cream having been fermented before churning. If this is not what you're going for, by all means use uncultured butter. Just save the salted butter for slathering on your bread.

Where a recipe calls for the butter and sugar to be creamed together, have the butter very soft, almost to the point of melting. This allows the butter and sugar to emulsify more smoothly. It will also help with emulsifying your room-temperature eggs.

A lot of **cream** that is sold in Australia is made with stabilisers, gums and thickeners. It's inexpensive and stable, with a long shelf life that's perfect for the major supermarkets. However, it doesn't have the flavour of real cream, and when used in cooking the results are different, and often undesirable.

We only use real or pure cream with a fat content of 35–45 per cent. To ensure that you are using pure cream, check the ingredient list on the packaging. Pure cream should contain only one ingredient: cream. Avoid creams that include added stabilisers, emulsifiers or other additives.

Crème fraîche and **sour cream** are both wonderful additions to your baking, or simply dolloped on top to serve. Avoid light or reduced-fat versions, and look for a higher fat content of 35–45 per cent. In industrial settings, both are made with pasteurised milk inoculated with specific bacterial cultures, with the main difference being that crème fraîche is fattier and thicker, and sour cream is tangier, lower in fat, and has a more liquid texture. We only use **full cream (whole) milk** in our recipes.

Bicarbonate of soda (baking soda) and baking powder are natural chemical leavening agents that have been in use for many years, having replaced yeast in many traditional bakes.

Bicarbonate of soda produces carbon dioxide when it comes into contact with liquids and acid. The carbon dioxide creates little pockets of air in the batter or dough, which give a nice, light mouthfeel. It's good for bakes with naturally acidic ingredients like buttermilk, sour cream or citrus. Most of the gas is released immediately, so get your bake in the oven quickly after combining the wet and dry ingredients.

Baking powder is a combination of bicarbonate of soda, acidic salts and a small amount of starch to stabilise. In addition to an initial reaction when mixed with liquid, it also reacts to heat. It's better for doughs that are mixed ahead of time, because you'll still get some lift from the heat of the oven.

Buy bicarbonate of soda and baking powder in small amounts and use within six months, as they both lose leavening power with age.

There are two main types of dried yeast – instant and active. In this book we have used instant dried yeast for buns, babas, babkas and saffron cake. Active dried yeast is a dehydrated form of yeast that requires activation in a liquid, whereas instant dried yeast doesn't require rehydration and proofing in water before being added to the dry ingredients. It's more convenient to use and also benefits from a quicker activation (a bit counterintuitive, considering its name!).

Dried yeasts are generally easier to find, have a longer shelf life and are more convenient to store than fresh yeast. If you prefer using fresh yeast, convert 7 g (¼ oz) dried yeast to 15 g (½ oz) compressed fresh yeast.

Dutch-processed cocoa powder has been mixed with an alkalising agent to neutralise the natural acidity of cocoa. It has a lovely deep colour and is preferred for baking because it works better with baking powder, which is also neutral. Natural cocoa or cacao powder are paler and more acidic, so will affect the leavening of your batter.

Techniques

TEMPERING CHOCOLATE

Tempered chocolate has a beautiful glossy finish, and a satisfying snap when you bite or break it. Tempering requires precision, but it's much easier than you might think – you just need a good thermometer and some focus.

You can temper dark, milk or white chocolate. Use high-quality bars of chocolate or couverture chocolate. The latter melts more quickly due to a higher cocoa mass, and is normally available as large buttons. If using bars, finely chop the chocolate with a serrated knife, as it will melt more evenly. The method below uses 300 g (10½ oz) of chocolate.

Melt 200 g (7 oz) of chocolate over a double boiler or bain marie until it reaches 45–50°C (115–120°F) on a sugar thermometer. Remove from the heat and add another 100 g (3½ oz) of chocolate. Continue to monitor as you stir in the solid chocolate until you reach the temperature in the table below.

Dark chocolate	Milk chocolate	White chocolate
28–29°C (82–84°F)	27–28°C (81–82°F)	26–27°C (79–81°F)

Return it to the heat briefly, and watch the thermometer closely until it reaches the working temperature in the table below.

Dark chocolate	Milk chocolate	White chocolate
31–32°C (88–90°F)	29–30°C (84–86°F)	28–29°C (82–84°F)

Remove from the heat and use immediately.

Alternatively, you can make a cheat's temper by melting chocolate and then adding a fat like a neutral-flavoured oil or melted butter, without the need for a thermometer. Add 5 per cent of the chocolate weight of oil, i.e. 20 g (¾ oz) oil to 400 g (14 oz) chocolate. Once your chocolate is melted, stir it in well and use immediately.

STERILISING

Always sterilise jars before storing pickles, jams and chutneys; your preserves will last almost indefinitely in containers that are sterilised before use. To sterilise your jars, preheat the oven to a low heat, between 100–120°C (210–250°F). Wash the jars in hot soapy water and rinse thoroughly, then place the clean jars on a baking tray and put them in the oven for 20 minutes. Make sure your jars are completely dry and still warm when you fill them.

JAMMING

The jam-making techniques in *Seasons captured* can be used to jam many fruits. If you prefer a chunkier jam than the recipe creates, macerate the fruit with the sugar and lemon juice overnight before applying any heat. Because they're already well combined, they won't need as long on the heat, giving them less time to 'cook down' and lose their structure.

Use the 'plate test' to check the consistency of your jams before jarring them. To do this, put a small plate in the freezer before you start making your jam. Once the jam reaches 105°C (220°F) on your sugar thermometer and starts to make large bubbles rather than small foamy ones, turn off the heat and take the plate out of the freezer. Drop a little jam onto the plate and put it in the fridge for 1 minute, then check the consistency by running your finger through the jam. If the jam spreads over the plate where your finger was, it needs more time. If you are left with a clear line, it has reached the correct setting point and is ready for jarring.

CHOCOLATE CURLS OR FLAKES

To make chocolate curls for decorating cakes or tarts, pour your tempered chocolate onto a flat hard surface. You could use a small slab of marble and refrigerate it for a couple of hours before you start. At home we use our stone bench, which works well.

Spread the chocolate with a large palette knife then let it just set. Place a large flexible metal scraper or knife at an acute angle from the bench, and gently push towards the set chocolate to create a large cigar shape or curls. Gently set aside to cool for about 10 minutes.

You will get some pieces that don't curl – put these in an airtight container in the freezer for future use. They're great for covering cakes like the Black forest gateau on page 56. Carefully transfer your perfect curls to an airtight container and store them somewhere cool and dry until needed.

Slow down

Once you've chosen your bake, plan ahead. Make time to read through the recipe in full before you start. It saves time in the long run, averts potential disasters and will help you feel more confident. The most important thing is to just enjoy the process. Embrace mistakes and write down any alterations you make (or would like to make next time).

To create good aeration in your dough, resist the urge to crank the mixer and rush the process. Mixing for longer (say, 10–15 minutes) on a medium speed creates a thicker and more stable mixture and makes it easier to fold in the dry ingredients without the dough collapsing.

Baking is often considered a precise science, relying on accurate measurements and specific techniques. There is another valuable element that can elevate your baking skills: intuition. This applies especially to live items like sourdough baking, but regardless of what you're making, trusting your instincts in the kitchen can add a personal touch and enhance the overall experience. Use all your senses. Rely on cues such as golden edges or a toothpick coming out clean to determine doneness. The more you bake, the more you'll develop an intuitive understanding of the process. Over time, you'll learn to anticipate outcomes and make informed decisions without solely relying on a recipe.

Baking takes practice to master. Your intuition might lead you to create unique treats that don't fit the mould of a traditional recipe. Many famous recipes were the result of mistakes in weighing up or technique. So let go of perfection, enjoy the process and see where it leads you.

Seasons
harnessed

Foundational recipes

Pages 21–39

Baking is a craft and an act of creation. The alchemy in taking raw ingredients and transforming them into something sublime is endlessly fascinating, evidenced by the enormous popularity of baking shows and books, and the rise of the celebrity baker. This fascination is amplified by the rotation of produce available throughout the seasons. It sparks a sense of curiosity and playfulness, of boundless possibility.

As with any craft, baking requires understanding and practice. And like all creative pursuits, if you master the basics, your palette is limitless. There is always more to learn, especially when working with whole, seasonal ingredients. Here we have our repertoire of pastries for different uses. We encourage you to learn the basics, develop a sense for how different pastries feel, and then lean into your intuition. Change things up – try a rich rye base for apple pie in winter, a lighter one for fresh cream and raspberries in summer, or a spelt pastry to complement stone fruits, berries and more.

Different flours perform differently, and some dairy products have a higher water content than others. These variations can alter the outcome of your bakes. This is totally fine, and something that we must normalise and embrace. The homogenisation of foods that gives us products such as shelf-stable white flour robs us of flavour, nutrients and diversity, all essential to true enjoyment beyond the sugar buzz. It also increases our separation from the people who grow our food. These are problems that can be addressed by asking where your ingredients come from, who grew them and how they were handled.

There really is no comparison with homemade pastry. We encourage you to experiment with these recipes, to gain confidence working with fresh, wholegrain flours and to open your eyes to the endless options provided by the perfect base.

SEASONS ALTERED

You might notice a theme running through our recipes: we love to play with different wholegrain flours for nutrition, flavour and a bit of fun. It's important to approach cooking with a sense of playfulness and curiosity, and not to get too obsessed with making things perfect. Some of these recipes use wholegrain flours mixed with plain: a gateway to wholefood baking, if you like.

In general, pastries made with wholegrain flours won't be as light as those made with plain, but they will have superior flavour and a higher nutritional value, especially if the flour is fresh. The pastry goes from being a base to carry flavour, to a complementary component of the finished bake.

Wholegrain flours will also absorb more liquid than plain, and some flours will absorb more than others. If you find the dough too dry you can add extra liquid, 1 tablespoon at a time as you are completing your dough, until you have the correct consistency. Once you get the hang of it, you'll get a feel for making adjustments as required.

Our kid is obsessed with chocolate (not sure where she gets that from!), so we've included a chocolate variation for the puff pastry. Another string to your baking bow.

This pastry is mostly used for sweet tarts like the Baked custard tart (page 122) and the Chocolate tart (page 141). It's a versatile pastry that keeps well in the freezer, ready to use whenever inspiration strikes.

There is no water in this recipe, which means that you will have minimal shrinking. It holds its shape well and produces a beautiful crisp crust.

Makes 1 kg (2 lb 3 oz)

200 g (7 oz) unsalted butter, softened

200 g (7 oz) caster (superfine) sugar

110 g (4 oz) eggs (approximately 2 large eggs), at room temperature

500 g (1 lb 2 oz) plain (all-purpose) flour

3 g (¹⁄₁₀ oz/½ teaspoon) fine sea salt

In a stand mixer fitted with the paddle attachment, gently cream the butter and sugar until just smooth. You want to mix it on a low–medium speed to avoid bringing air into the pastry. Lightly whisk the eggs in a small bowl, and add to the mixer a little at a time until just combined, then add the flour and salt in two additions. Mix very gently for 10 seconds until the pastry just comes together.

Tip the pastry out onto a lightly floured bench, divide into two pieces and flatten each out into a disc 2 cm (¾ in) thick. Wrap and rest in the fridge for at least 1 hour, or until you're ready to use it. Sweet pastry will keep in the fridge for a week, and up to 3 months in the freezer wrapped well in plastic wrap or in a container.

Flaky pastry

If you only ever make one type of pastry, make it this one. It's endlessly handy for both sweet and savoury baking, is super easy to make and is exceptionally forgiving to *hand-grenade hands* (a technical term for careless or inexperienced bakers).

This flaky pastry is also extremely adaptable. We have included variations for different grains – buckwheat is deeply flavourful and works well with chocolate, and is also delicious used in the Apple and buckwheat pie (page 152). Buckwheat is also an important 'fallow' crop for wheat growers, and we should all be eating more of it to support our farmers.

You can also change out the liquid – try crème fraîche or milk kefir instead of water for a bit of zing. Try making the plain dough first, so you get to know how it should feel, then once you're comfortable with that, you can change the flours and liquids used, knowing what you're aiming for.

Makes 700 g (1 lb 9 oz)

225 g (8 oz) unsalted butter, chilled
350 g (12½ oz) plain
     (all-purpose) flour
5 g (⅛ oz) fine sea salt
120 g (4½ oz) cold water

Wholemeal (whole-wheat) variation

225 g (8 oz) unsalted butter, chilled
250 g (9 oz) wholemeal (whole
     wheat) or spelt flour
100 g (3½ oz) plain
     (all-purpose) flour
5 g (⅛ oz) fine sea salt
140 g (5 oz) cold water

Whole rye variation

225 g (8 oz) unsalted butter, chilled
180 g (6½ oz) rye flour or
     wholegrain rye flour
170 g (6 oz) plain (all-purpose) flour
5 g (⅛ oz) fine sea salt
140 g (5 oz) cold water

Buckwheat variation

225 g (8 oz) unsalted butter, chilled
180 g (6½ oz) buckwheat flour
170 g (6 oz) plain (all-purpose) flour
5 g (⅛ oz) fine sea salt
140 g (5 oz) cold water

Cut the butter into 1 cm (½ in) dice and chill it in the freezer while you weigh up the rest of your ingredients.

Put the flour and salt in a mound on your kitchen bench and scatter the chilled butter cubes over the top. Use a rolling pin to roll the butter into the flour, gathering the flour back into the middle as you go with a dough scraper. Keep rolling until the mixture has a crumbly texture, with pea-sized lumps or shards of butter still visible.

Make a well in the middle, and add the water. Use a dough scraper or spoon to gently cut the flour into the water until you have an even crumbly texture, gathering up any leaks as you do.

Use your fingertips to gently push it all together into a rough dough, with a slightly sticky texture. If it feels dry, add more water, 1 tablespoon at a time, until there are no floury bits left.

Roll or press the dough out into a rectangle roughly 2–3 cm (¾–1¼ in) thick (exact dimensions are not important here). Fold one-third of the dough into the middle, then the other third over the top of that, as if folding a letter. Rotate the dough 90 degrees and roll it out again, into a rectangle roughly 2–3 cm (¾–1¼ in) thick, then repeat the letter fold. Don't worry about making these folds perfectly neat – this is just to finish bringing the dough together and layering the butter, which results in a lovely flakiness. If the dough is still a bit dry or floury, add a bit more water as you go.

Rotate and roll out the dough once more into a rectangle 2–3 cm (¾–1¼ in) thick and do one last fold. Wrap and refrigerate for at least 1 hour, or overnight. It will keep for 4–5 days in the fridge, or for up to 3 months in the freezer.

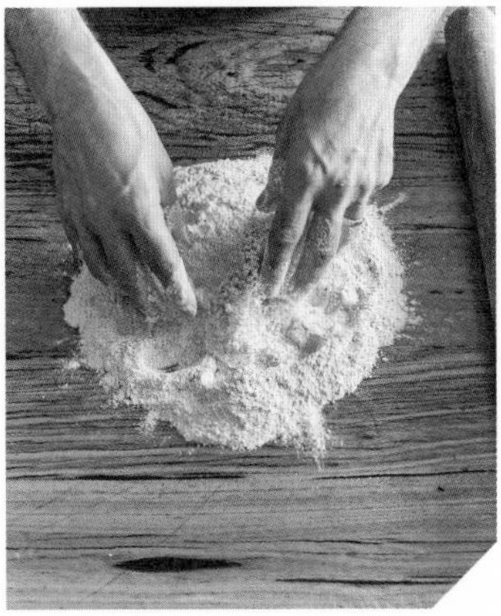
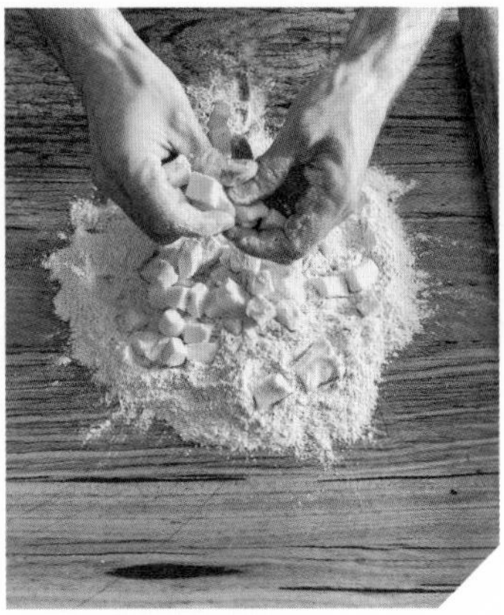
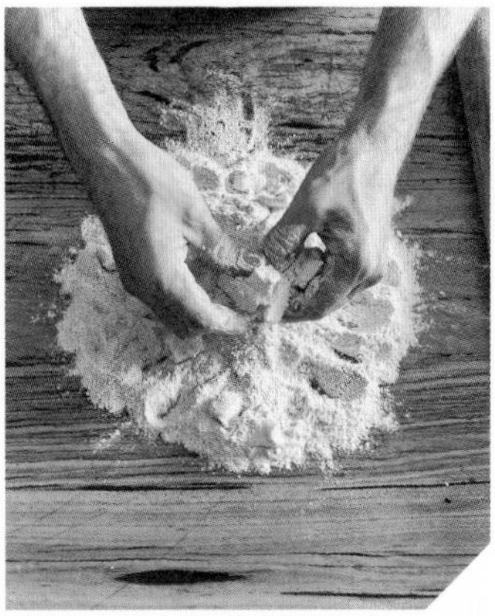
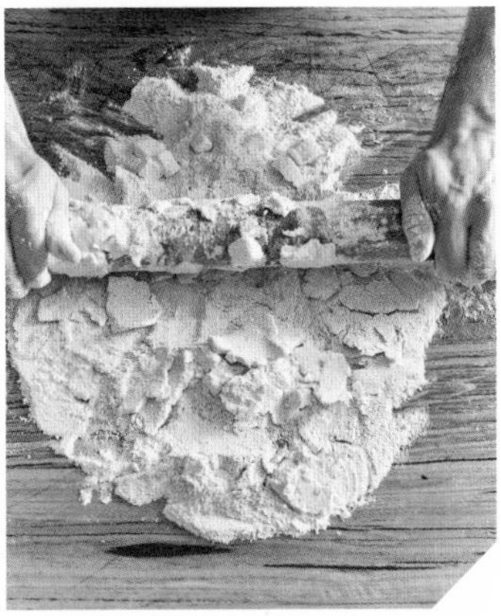
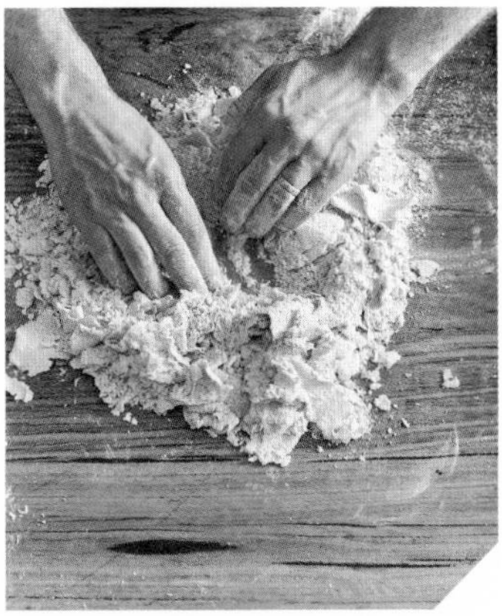
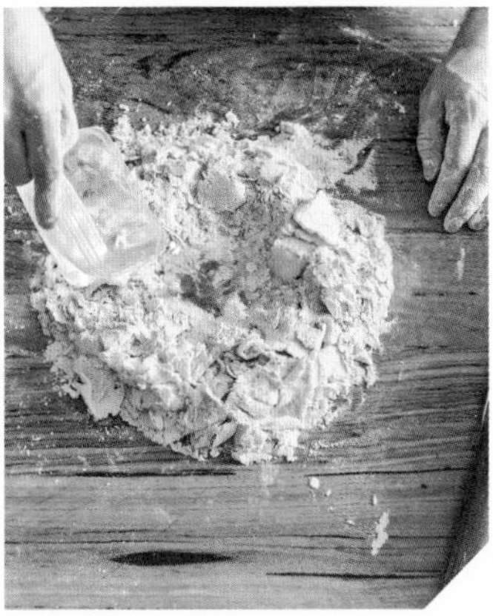
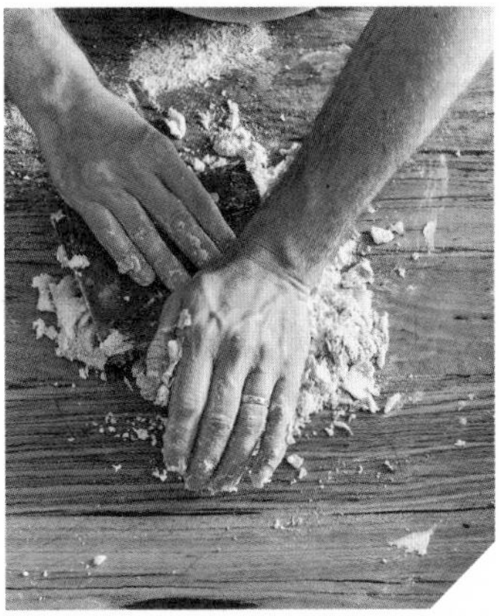
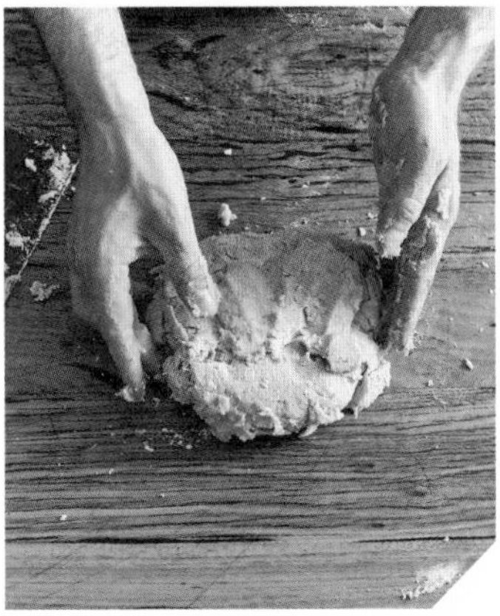
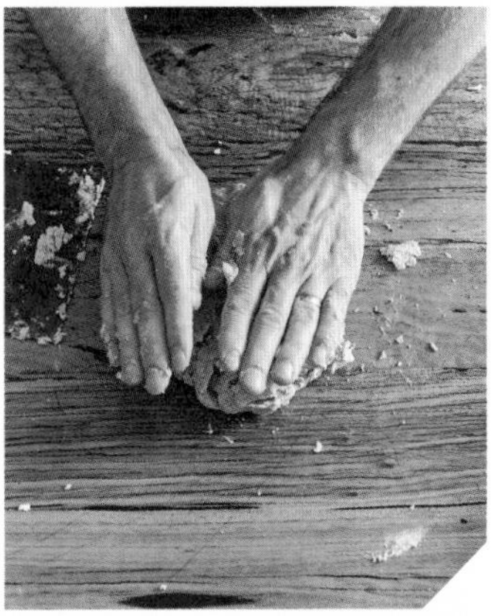
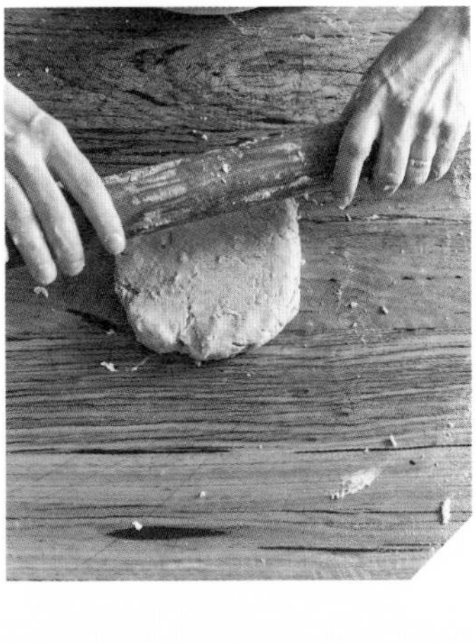
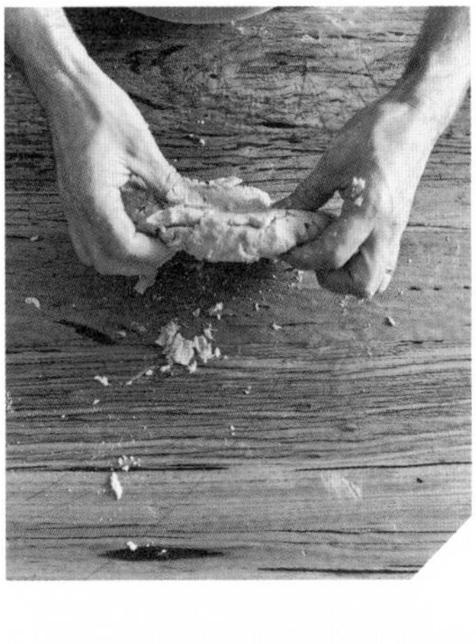
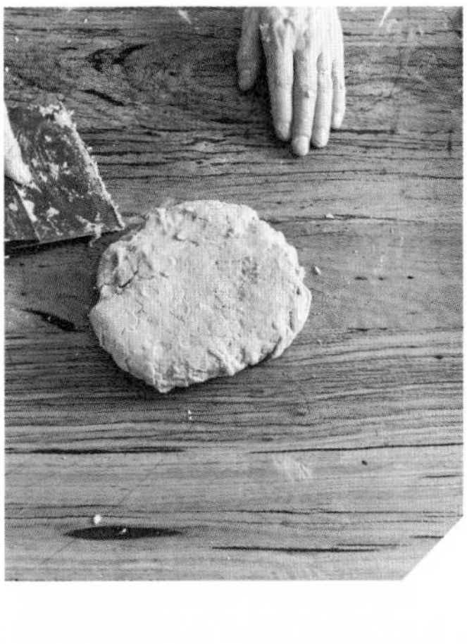

Vegan flaky pastry

This pastry will create a delicious, flaky and highly useful base for all your tarts and galettes. Making your own vegan butter might seem like a step too far, but the result will provide the flakiness you're after and is worth the effort. Break up the steps by making the vegan butter a day before you make the pastry. Nutritional yeast provides a nice colour and a gentle umami flavour, but the pastry will work fine without it.

There are solid, valid reasons to choose a vegan diet. If you (or someone you love) has chosen veganism, you (or they) undoubtedly have a good heart and have thought deeply about the impacts food choices can have on your health and on Earth.

But ... choosing veganism doesn't excuse you from confronting the industrial food complex and its impacts. Supermarkets have whole aisles dedicated to highly processed and excessively packaged vegan foods. These foods are no less harmful than other industrially produced foods, and quite possibly worse than non-vegan foods raised and prepared with care. Veganism is not the convenient way to appease climate or animal cruelty guilt that it's sometimes marketed as. Which is why you need to have a great non-industrial vegan pastry recipe to hand – and here it is!

Makes 800 g (1 lb 12 oz)

Vegan butter

160 g (5½ oz) refined deodorised coconut oil

30 g (1 oz) light olive oil

50 g (1¾ oz) soy or other plant-based milk

4 g (⅛ oz) apple-cider vinegar

2 g (¹⁄₁₆ oz/1½ teaspoons) nutritional yeast (optional)

Pastry

400 g (14 oz) plain (all-purpose) flour

8 g (¼ oz) fine sea salt

240 g (8½ oz) vegan butter (see above), chilled and cut into 1 cm (½ in) dice

150 g (5½ oz) chilled plant-based milk or water

To make the vegan butter, melt the coconut oil in a small saucepan over a low heat until just melted. Take the pan off the heat and whisk in the olive oil, milk, vinegar and nutritional yeast, if using. Set aside, occasionally whisking the mixture until it cools and forms a thick paste. Refrigerate in a sealed container overnight.

To make the pastry, combine the flour, salt and diced butter in the bowl of a stand mixer fitted with the paddle attachment. Mix on a medium speed until well combined. You should still see pea-sized shards of butter.

With the mixer running, add the liquid and mix for another 30–60 seconds, until the dough just comes together. The dough should not be sticky and you should still see pieces of butter.

Turn the pastry out onto a lightly floured bench and fold it a few times to help build up layers. To do this, take half of the dough and pull it up and over itself, then push down on it. Repeat this a few times and then shape the dough into a slab. Wrap and refrigerate for at least 1 hour, or overnight.

Roll the pastry between two sheets of baking paper to the required shape and thickness, then wrap and return it to the fridge for 1 hour before using. Allowing the butter to set into the pastry will give you a flakier result.

This pastry will keep for 1 week in the fridge or 3 months in the freezer.

Most pastry relies on the stretch and strength of gluten protein bonds for texture. There is no gluten-free seed or grain that can successfully replicate this, so instead, we use a mixture of flours that each perform a different task in bringing the dough together.

To achieve the desired flaky texture, we laminate a butter sheet into the dough, similar to the technique used to make puff pastry. Try to keep the dough temperature stable so the butter is soft enough to work with but doesn't melt into the dough as you laminate. You'll find these ingredients in bulk food stores online or at local health food shops.

This dough can be used for pies, tarts, galettes and more.

Makes 1 kg (2 lb 3 oz)

90 g (3 oz) tapioca starch

90 g (3 oz) potato starch

20 g (¾ oz) pea or soy flour

140 g (5 oz) brown rice flour (plus extra for dusting)

70 g (2½ oz) sorghum flour

10 g (⅓ oz) xanthan gum

7 g (¼ oz) fine sea salt

100 g (3½ oz) cold unsalted butter, cut into 1 cm (½ in) dice

230 g (8 oz) water

250 g (9 oz) chilled unsalted butter, for laminating

Combine the tapioca starch, potato starch, pea or soy flour, brown rice flour, sorghum flour, xanthan gum and salt in a large bowl, and mix well. Scatter over the chilled diced butter and use your hands to work it into the dry ingredients until the mixture looks like breadcrumbs. Add the water and continue mixing with your hands, bringing it all together into firm dough with the texture of playdough. It should have a slight stickiness; if it feels too dry, add more water, 1 tablespoon at a time, incorporating it fully between additions.

Tip the dough out onto a lightly floured kitchen bench and knead it for 3–4 minutes, then shape it into a rectangle about 18 × 20 cm (7 × 8 in). Cover and refrigerate the dough for 2 hours, or overnight.

While the dough is cooling, prepare the butter block for laminating. Place the butter block between two sheets of baking paper and use a rolling pin to roll it into a rectangle about 18 × 20 cm (7 × 8 in). Put the butter in the fridge, between the sheets of baking paper, until you're ready to laminate your pastry.

Remove the butter and dough from the fridge 15 minutes before laminating, so it can soften slightly. Dust your bench with brown rice flour, then lay the dough rectangle on the bench with the short side closest to you. Roll the dough away from you until you have a rectangle 20 × 40 cm (8 × 15¾ in), still with the short side closest to you.

Place the butter block in the middle of the dough, with the shorter edge closest to you and a 1 cm (½ in) margin on each side. Fold both free short sides of the dough over the top of the butter so they meet in the middle, encasing the butter. Lightly pinch the ends together to seal (the seam should run parallel with the bench).

Rotate the dough block 90 degrees so the seam is now perpendicular to the edge of the bench. Roll the dough away from you until you have a rectangle 20 × 40 cm (8 × 15¾ in), with the shortest edge closest to you. Fold the bottom third of the dough up over the butter, and then the top third down over the top of that, as if folding a letter. Rotate the dough 90 degrees anticlockwise, placing the open seam to the right. Repeat this step three more times, rotating the dough 90 degrees between each fold.

There's no need to rest the dough between folds; there is no gluten in the flour, so the dough will not shrink. However, you do need to be careful that the butter doesn't get too soft. If it starts to feel soft, put it in the fridge for 30 minutes after the second fold before proceeding.

Once all four folds are done, wrap your dough and chill for at least 1 hour before use. Leave the dough at room temperature for 15 minutes before use, to soften slightly. It will keep for 5 days in the fridge, or up to 3 months in the freezer, well wrapped.

Puff pastry

Many people think puff pastry is too hard to make themselves. You do need to have an awareness of touch and temperature, but the steps are fairly simple. Please, have a go! Our top tip is to break the tasks down into simple steps and have a rest yourself in between each one.

Makes 830 g (1 lb 13 oz)

70 g (2½ oz) unsalted butter, chilled

150 g (5½ oz) chilled water

10 g (⅓ oz/2 teaspoons) white vinegar

340 g (12 oz) plain (all-purpose) flour, plus extra for dusting

10 g (⅓ oz) fine sea salt

For laminating

250 g (9 oz) block unsalted butter, at room temperature

Wholemeal (whole-wheat) variation

70 g (2½ oz) unsalted butter, chilled

180 g (6½ oz) chilled water

10 g (⅓ oz/2 teaspoons) white vinegar

170 g (6 oz) wholemeal (whole-wheat) flour

170 g (6 oz) plain (all-purpose) flour

10 g (⅓ oz) fine sea salt

Chocolate variation

70 g (2½ oz) unsalted butter, chilled

180 g (6½ oz) chilled water

10 g (⅓ oz/2 teaspoons) white vinegar

310 g (11 oz) plain (all-purpose) flour

40 g (1½ oz) cocoa powder

10 g (⅓ oz) fine sea salt

Day 1

Take the butter out of the fridge, cut it into 1 cm (½ in) cubes and leave to soften slightly for 10 minutes – you want it to be cold, but pliable.

Combine the water and vinegar in a jug. Put the flour (and cocoa, if making the chocolate variation), salt and butter cubes into the bowl of a stand mixer fitted with the paddle attachment and mix on medium speed to break the butter into the flour until you have pea–sized lumps of butter still visible. With the mixer still running, pour in the vinegar mixture and mix until the dough just comes together. You don't want any dry pieces, but you need to be careful not to overwork the dough.

Flatten the dough into a rectangle about 1 cm (½ in) thick. Wrap the dough and rest it in the fridge overnight.

Meanwhile, prepare the butter for laminating. Lay the butter block between two sheets of baking paper and use a rolling pin to roll it into a rectangle about 18 × 20 cm (7 × 8 in). Leave the butter between the sheets of baking paper and refrigerate overnight, along with the dough. Sleep well, knowing that you're on your way to homemade puff!

Day 2

Remove the dough and rolled-out butter from the fridge about 30 minutes before laminating. You want the butter to be malleable but not too soft.

Keep your bench well dusted with flour, as the dough can be quite sticky. Lay the dough rectangle on the bench with the short side closest to you. Roll the dough away from you to form a rectangle 20 × 40 cm (8 × 15¾ in), with the short side closest to you.

Place the butter block in the centre of the dough rectangle, with the 20 cm (8 in) side of the butter parallel with the bench. Fold both free short sides of the dough over the top of the butter so they meet in the middle, encasing the butter. Lightly pinch the ends together to seal (the seam should run parallel with the bench).

Rotate the block 90 degrees so the seam is now perpendicular to the edge of the bench. Roll the dough away from you to form a 20 × 40 cm (8 × 15¾ in) rectangle, again with the short side closest to you. Fold the bottom third of the dough into the middle, then the top third over the top of that, as if folding a letter. Refrigerate for 20 minutes.

Put your dough on the bench with the open seam on your right-hand side and perpendicular to the edge of the bench. Roll the dough away from you to form a rectangle 20 × 40 cm (8 × 15¾ in) long. Fold the bottom third of the dough into the middle, then the top third over the top of that, as if folding a letter. Repeat this step until you have completed four single (or letter) folds in total. Refrigerate your dough for 20 minutes after two folds to keep the butter from getting too soft (or after every fold if it's a warm day).

Once all four folds are done, wrap your pastry and rest it in the fridge for at least 6 hours, preferably overnight, before you use it. Chilling the pastry before use prevents it from shrinking. When you're ready to use it, roll it out to whatever thickness you need. The pastry will keep for 3–4 days in the fridge, or up to 1 month in the freezer.

Sablé means sand in French, a reference to the texture of the cooked pastry here. This pastry is lighter and flakier than the flaky pastry, making a lovely, biscuity base for a little cream and fruit. It's also a little trickier to work with, in that it is more delicate to roll out and hold together, but the result is a wonderfully light and crumbly texture once baked. Both the flavour and texture are worth the effort. Promise.

The wholemeal version of this pastry is used in the Pistachio and raspberry wagon wheels (page 118).

Makes 680 g (1½ lb)

285 g (10 oz) unsalted butter, softened

110 g (4 oz) icing (confectioners') sugar, sifted

½ vanilla bean, seeds scraped (or ½ teaspoon vanilla paste)

285 g (10 oz) plain (all-purpose) flour

¼ teaspoon fine sea salt

Wholemeal (whole-wheat) variation

285 g (10 oz) unsalted butter

110 g (4 oz) icing (confectioners') sugar, sifted

½ vanilla bean, seeds scraped (or ½ teaspoon vanilla paste)

285 g (10 oz) wholemeal (whole-wheat) flour

¼ teaspoon fine sea salt

In a stand mixer fitted with the paddle attachment, gently cream together the butter, icing sugar and vanilla until you have a smooth paste. Be careful not to incorporate air into the mixture. In a medium-sized bowl, whisk the flour and salt together, then add to the creamed butter mixture in three increments, beating slowly with the paddle attachment between each addition. After the third addition, mix until just combined – there should be no flour visible.

Tip the dough out onto a lightly floured bench, divide into two pieces and flatten each out into a disc 2 cm (¾ in) thick. Wrap each disc and rest in the fridge for at least 1 hour before using.

Sablé pastry will keep in the fridge for 1 week, and in the freezer for up to 3 months.

Choux pastry

Handling choux pastry requires skill. For perfect aeration when baked, use a nice strong flour that can hold the structure. The pastry is piped, which also takes practice. Perhaps don't make choux for the first time when the stakes are high, but do give it a go. It's something different, so satisfying and has many different uses, from eclairs and profiteroles to French crullers.

Top tips: weigh out your eggs, as the sizes vary enormously, and you need precision here. Fix any wonky shapes or messy bits with wet hands prior to baking, and whatever you do, don't open the oven door during the initial phase of the bake. A blast of cold air in the oven chamber will deflate your choux, and your pride.

It's best to bake this dough on the day that you mix it, so check your recipe and preheat the oven before you start on the dough. Once baked, your choux shapes can be frozen and then re-baked to form a lovely golden crust.

Makes 700 g (1 lb 9 oz)

250 g (9 oz) water
25 g (1 oz) caster (superfine) sugar
80 g (2¾ oz) unsalted butter
3 g (⅒ oz) fine sea salt
150 g (5½ oz) bakers (strong) flour
200 g (7 oz) eggs, at room
   temperature, lightly whisked

Combine the water, sugar, butter and salt in a medium saucepan. Bring to a simmer over a medium heat, stirring to dissolve the sugar and salt. Add the flour and mix well with a wooden spoon. Stir continuously over a medium heat for 2–3 minutes until it all comes together in a slightly sticky, thick paste.

Transfer to a stand mixer fitted with the paddle attachment and beat on medium–high speed for 30 seconds before slowly adding the eggs. Continue to mix until fully incorporated. The dough should be shiny and smooth, and ready to pipe into your preferred shape. The dough will keep in the fridge for 3 days, but for best results, shape and bake the dough the day it's mixed.

Wholemeal shortbread

Shortbread is – shamelessly – all about butter. We like to use a local cultured butter, which gives the biscuit depth and complexity. Using wholemeal flour also adds depth of flavour, resulting in a biscuit that doesn't need to be dunked in a cup of tea to be enjoyed.

The aroma of great butter and wholemeal flour baking together is pretty magical, reminiscent of baking at home for people we love. Aside from being enjoyed on its own or with a cuppa, shortbread is great with a rich creamy dish such as Lemon posset (page 64) or Warm pudding with berry compote (page 67).

Makes about 600 g (1 lb 5 oz)

230 g (8 oz) unsalted butter, softened

115 g (4 oz) raw (demerara) sugar

1 vanilla bean, seeds scraped (or 1 teaspoon vanilla paste)

250 g (9 oz) wholemeal (whole-wheat) flour

50 g (1¾ oz) cornflour (cornstarch)

½ teaspoon fine sea salt

caster (superfine) sugar, for sprinkling

In a stand mixer fitted with the paddle attachment, cream together the butter, sugar and vanilla on a medium speed for about 5 minutes, until pale and creamy.

Sift together the flour, cornflour and salt. The main objective here is to mix them well. The bran particles won't go through the sieve – don't discard them, just add them back in and mix well. Add the flour mixture to the creamed butter mixture in three increments, beating slowly between each addition. After the third addition, mix until just combined.

Tip the dough out onto a lightly floured bench and gently knead, just to bring it all together. Wrap the dough and rest it in the fridge for at least 1 hour before using, or preferably overnight.

When you're ready to bake, preheat the oven to 160°C (320°F). Line a baking tray with baking paper.

Place the dough on a lightly floured bench. Use a rolling pin to roll it into a rectangle 20 × 15 cm (8 × 6 in), and 1.5 cm (½ in) thick. Cut it into 2 × 10 cm (¾ × 4 in) fingers.

Space your shortbread fingers out onto the baking tray and bake for 15 minutes. Rotate the tray in the oven and bake for another 2–5 minutes, until the edges are just starting to colour. Remove from the oven and sprinkle with caster sugar to finish. Cool on a wire rack before eating (although they're lovely when still warm).

The baked shortbread will keep in an airtight container for up to 5 days.

Brioche loaf

It's worth making brioche just to experience the aromas that fill your kitchen as it comes out of the oven. Use it for delicious Plum bostock (page 116), or the ultimate French toast. To achieve a light, soft texture, keep the dough temperature at around 22–24°C (72–75°F) as you mix and prove it. This can all be done on the same day, or you can make the dough the day before and leave it to slow prove in the fridge overnight. Once baked, the brioche keeps well for a few days in an airtight container. It also freezes well – either toast it from frozen or refresh it in the oven for 6 minutes at 160°C (320°F).

Makes 660 g (1 lb 7 oz)

320 g (11½ oz) bakers (strong) flour
40 g (1½ oz) soft brown sugar
5 g (⅛ oz) fine sea salt
150 g (5½ oz/3 medium) eggs,
    at room temperature
60 g (2 oz) full-cream (whole) milk
7 g (¼ oz/2 teaspoons) instant dried
    yeast or 15 g (½ oz) fresh yeast
80 g (2¾ oz) unsalted butter, at
    room temperature, cut into
    1 cm (½ in) dice

Egg wash

1 egg
splash of full-cream (whole) milk
pinch of fine sea salt

Put the flour, sugar, salt, eggs, milk and yeast in the mixing bowl of a stand mixer fitted with the dough hook. Mix on low speed for 5 minutes to incorporate the ingredients, stopping occasionally to scrape down the side of the bowl. Check the consistency – it should be like slightly sticky playdough.

Increase the speed to medium and mix for a further 5 minutes, then add the butter all at once. Continue to mix on medium speed for another 8 minutes, scraping down the side of the bowl a few times. Mix until your dough comes away from the side of the bowl and is velvety and smooth; you should be able to stretch it out without it breaking.

Cover and set aside for 1 hour, ideally at around 22–24°C (72–75°F), to allow the dough to rise. If it is too cold, put the dough in your (cold) oven with the light on, with a pan of hot water at the bottom to create warmth and humidity.

After 1 hour, give the dough a fold. Wet or oil your hands and grab a piece of dough on the side of the bowl. Pull and stretch it up over the middle to the other side of the bowl. Repeat this 6–8 times, working around the bowl. You can also knead the dough on the benchtop.

Cover once more and set aside at room temperature to prove for another hour or so, until the dough has risen and feels light and full of air – it should wobble a little when you gently shake the bowl. To check, gently poke the dough. If your fingertip leaves a dent, it's ready – if the dough springs back quickly, cover it again and give it more time.

Once the dough is ready, shape, prove and bake your brioche. Lightly grease a 12 × 23 cm (4¾ × 9 in), 7 cm (2¾ in) deep, straight-sided loaf tin. Tip your fully proved brioche dough onto a lightly floured kitchen bench and divide it into three equal pieces, about 220 g (8 oz) each.

Shape each piece of dough into a tight ball. To do this, take one piece and knock out any large bubbles, then gently pull the edges out and fold them over in the middle. Turn it over so the seam is underneath. Place your dominant hand over the dough and push it down as you move your hand in a circular motion, rotating the dough under your palm.

You may find it easier to cup both hands around the dough. Applying pressure as you shape each piece builds strength in the dough and makes it tauter. This process should take about 30 seconds. Repeat with the remaining two pieces, then put the three balls in the tin, smooth side up.

Cover and set aside to prove, ideally at 22–24°C (72–75°F) for 1–1½ hours. After 1 hour, preheat the oven to 170°C (340°F). If your dough is ready but your oven is not quite up to temperature, put the tin in the fridge until you are ready to bake.

Make the egg wash by lightly whisking the egg, milk and salt together.

Just before baking, lightly brush the top of the dough with egg wash, or spray it with water. Bake on the top shelf of the oven for 25–30 minutes, turning the tin halfway through to ensure an even bake. To test if the loaf is ready, remove it from the tin and tap the bottom. If it sounds hollow, it's ready. Cool in the tin on a wire rack.

Almond frangipane

Nuts are a wonderful baking staple, and frangipane is such a simple ingredient to create satisfying bakes with great depth of flavour. Almond frangipane is just the start – you can also use other nuts for their different flavours. The combination of pistachio and almond is delicious, and the vibrant pistachio green looks stunning.

Nuts will oxidise quickly once ground, losing flavour and nutrition. For this reason, we always buy whole nuts and grind them ourselves. Our preference is to leave the skin on, for more flavour and texture. Blitz them in your food processor, and for best results store your nuts in the fridge or freezer. Grinding from cold means they won't heat up as quickly, resulting in a finer meal. Blitz them for long enough to create a fine meal, but not so long that you create nut butter.

Because of the high fat content, frangipane sets fairly solid when cold. Take it out of the fridge well before you assemble your bake – it will be much easier to work with at room temperature.

If you make a little more than you need, transfer the rest to a container and freeze it for up to 3 months. It's great for emergency bakes!

Makes 1 kg (2 lb 3 oz)

230 g (8 oz) unsalted butter, softened

285 g (10 oz) caster (superfine) sugar

1 vanilla bean, seeds scraped (or 1 teaspoon vanilla paste)

grated zest of 1 lemon

285 g (10 oz) ground almonds

50 g (1¾ oz) plain (all-purpose) flour

5 medium eggs, at room temperature

In a stand mixer fitted with the paddle attachment, cream together butter, sugar, vanilla and lemon zest on a medium speed until pale and fluffy. Combine ground almonds and flour in a bowl and whisk with a fork to knock out any lumps. Lightly whisk the eggs in a separate bowl.

Add the eggs to the creamed butter mixture in several increments, with the paddle still going, ensuring that each addition is fully incorporated before adding the next. Once the eggs are completely incorporated, add the dry ingredients and mix with the paddle until just combined.

Transfer to a container and refrigerate until you're ready to use.

Seasons past

Nostalgic indulgence

Pages 41–67

Baking can arouse some profound sentimental reflection. The smells that emanate from the oven during a bake fill the home and create sensory memories. Years later, these transport us back in time, sparking memories of loved ones gathering to enjoy the fruits of the season. In this way, we create ritual and tradition that is unique to the places where we live.

The significance of the hereditary bakes we have included in this chapter is not lost on us, and we are intentionally carrying them forward for our daughter. She is growing up on the opposite side of the world from where Michael was raised, and these traditional Cornish bakes are a way of tethering her to that incredible place. She loves to hear stories from both sides of the family, giving her a sense of belonging and connection. She knows that her maternal Granny was a star baker back in the day, and is fully focused when given the opportunity to bake with her. She listens closely when Pippa resurrects a recipe and speaks of its origin. And many of these recipes are quite simple, offering an ideal opportunity to get children involved in the kitchen.

Cornish saffron cake is particularly nostalgic for Michael. His great-grandparents grew saffron crocus flowers. His uncle Paul tells of licking the bowls as he waited for the cake to come out of the oven, of how saffron is his 'safe smell'. Heavy cake is another great Cornish bake, shared here with pride. The ginger fairings have been reverse engineered to be reminiscent of the biscuits sold in packets throughout Cornwall. Warming and flavourful, they always go down a treat.

You will also find adaptable staples here. Digestive biscuits, served savoury or sweet, a reliable sponge cake, and universal favourites like carrot cake and the ultimate black forest gateau.

We tell stories through food. Through these stories we learn about our ancestors, about the turning of the seasons, and we gain connection to the natural world. So much about our global food systems creates disconnection. From the stories of the farmers growing our fruit, to the stories of our grandmothers, if we choose to lean in and listen, we have much to gain. We've seen global systems falter through the COVID-19 pandemic and increasing climate disasters. Sharing and hearing food stories can create broader access to safe and culturally appropriate foods, and increase community-based resilience in a changing world.

Through these recipes we ultimately hope to share with you our joy in baking. We hope that you will create your own classics and your own memories with your chosen families. These recipes are achievable and fun, no matter your background. Please join us in exploring our pasts, to create some things to make sense of our present.

Heavy cake

Heavy cake – sometimes called Hevva cake – was traditionally made by Cornish fishermen's wives to welcome their husbands home from sea. It became widely known throughout the county, baked by countless grannies for afternoon tea. Rich with fruit and lard, it's the perfect treat for a drizzly Cornish afternoon with the wind blowing in off the sea. The lattice scoring on top of the cake represents a fishing net, a symbol to celebrate a successful catch and offer luck to the fishermen on their next journey at sea.

This is one of the easiest cakes you can make – it's almost like a giant scone. It's perfect for when you are in a hurry, and no machines or mixers are needed. The smell of this Heavy cake in the oven brings back fond memories of family gatherings, and days of friends and family popping in unannounced. If you want the house to smell amazing when your guests arrive, make the cake in advance and keep it in the fridge, then bake it just before serving. Yum!

This recipe comes from Michael's beloved great aunt, Alison Noall.

SEASONS ALTERED

We've gone with tradition here, and used lard. If you prefer, you could use 250 g (9 oz) unsalted butter instead. You could also use different dried fruits, or a mixture.

Serves 8–10

450 g (1 lb) plain (all-purpose) flour
2 teaspoons baking powder
85 g (3 oz) raw (demerara) sugar
110 g (4 oz) unsalted butter, chilled and cut into 2 cm (¾ in) cubes
140 g (5 oz) lard, chilled and cut into 2 cm (¾ in) cubes
200 g (7 oz) currants
1 teaspoon fine sea salt
250 g (9 oz) full-cream (whole) milk
1 egg, at room temperature
raw (demerara) sugar, for dusting

Egg wash

1 egg
splash of full-cream (whole) milk
pinch of fine sea salt

Preheat the oven to 180°C (360°F). Line a baking tray with baking paper.

Combine the flour, baking powder, sugar and salt in a medium mixing bowl. Use your fingers to gently toss it all together, then add the butter and lard. Rub the fats into the flour mixture until you have a rough crumble with pea-sized lumps of butter and lard still visible. Add the currants and toss them through.

Lightly whisk the milk and egg together, add to the dry ingredients and mix until just combined – you don't want any flour visible, but you do still want to see the lumps of butter and lard.

Make the egg wash by lightly whisking the egg, milk and salt together.

Transfer the dough to your lined baking tray and push it into a large oval shape. Use a rolling pin to roll it out until it's about 3 cm (1¼ in) high and the top surface is even. Use a knife to score the top into a lattice pattern, then brush the top and sides with egg wash and sprinkle with demerara sugar.

Bake on the top shelf of the oven for 20 minutes, then check that it's baking evenly. Rotate the tray in the oven and bake for another 6–8 minutes, or until you have a nice even golden colour.

This cake is so good served warm with a cup of tea, and will keep for 3–4 days at room temperature in an airtight container.

Cornish saffron cake

Saffron was introduced to Cornwall by Spanish traders, who exchanged it for tin. Over many years it became ubiquitous across the county – so much so that for the Cornish, saffron is more a home comfort than an exotic wonder. Powerfully aromatic and beautifully coloured, it's one of Michael's favourite spices, and Cornish saffron cake is a bake that never fails to remind him of home.

This old-fashioned yeasted cake was almost a permanent feature at Michael's grandparents' home, kept on hand for unexpected visitors. It keeps well and is lovely toasted with some butter, the aromas enveloping you like a hug as it warms. It's also not too sweet, making it ideal for morning or afternoon tea.

Handling the yeasted dough can feel a bit more like bread making than cake making, in that it's rested repeatedly and is shaped before being transferred into the tin. If these techniques are unfamiliar, try viewing this recipe as a learning opportunity. Perhaps it will be the start of a whole new baking journey!

SEASONS ALTERED

Different dried fruits will work in place of the mixed peel. Some old recipes use sultanas.

Makes two 25 × 10 cm (10 × 4 in) loaf cakes

350 g (12½ oz) full-cream (whole) milk

1 g (⅟₃₂ oz) saffron threads

25 g (1 oz) fresh yeast or 12 g (½ oz) instant dried yeast

450 g (1 lb) bakers (strong) flour

60 g (2 oz) soft brown sugar

½ teaspoon fine sea salt

120 g (4½ oz) unsalted butter, at room temperature, cut into 1 cm (½ in) dice

100 g (3½ oz) currants

50 g (1¾ oz) mixed peel

½ teaspoon freshly grated nutmeg

½ teaspoon ground cinnamon

Combine the milk and saffron in a small saucepan over a medium heat. Slowly bring it up to a simmer, being careful not to let it boil. Remove from the heat and set aside to cool to room temperature.

Mix the yeast with 50 g (1¾ oz) of the saffron-infused milk and 50 g (1¾ oz) of the flour in a small bowl and leave it to activate for 15–20 minutes.

In a stand mixer fitted with the dough hook, combine the remaining milk with the remaining flour and the sugar and salt. Mix on medium speed for 2–3 minutes, until well combined. Add the activated yeast mixture and mix for 8–10 minutes on medium speed, scraping down the side of the bowl with a dough scraper or spatula halfway through.

When the dough is well formed, add the butter in two or three additions, continuing to mix on medium speed. Once the butter is fully incorporated, add the dried fruit and spices and mix well until they're evenly distributed through the dough. Turn the dough out onto your benchtop and knead it with your hands to bring everything together. Lightly oil the sides of a large bowl and place the dough inside. Cover with a clean tea towel and leave to rest in a warm place (ideally around 22–24°C/72–75°F) to prove for 30 minutes.

Turn the dough out onto your benchtop again and knead it for 30 seconds or so, to knock it back and ensure the dried fruit is well distributed. Return it to the bowl and cover for another 30 minutes.

Grease and line two 25 × 10 cm (10 × 4 in) loaf tins.

Tip the dough onto your benchtop and cut it into two even pieces. Shape each piece into a rectangle with a short edge that matches the length of your loaf tins. Place the short edge closest to you and roll the dough into a log, starting at the top of the rectangle and rolling towards you. To do this, fold over a small piece at the top and press it down a little, then roll that over again and press it down gently. Continue rolling like this until you get to the end, and use the heel of your hand to seal any gaps.

Put each log into one of your prepared tins, with the seam side down. Leave covered in a warm place to prove for 1 hour.

Preheat the oven to 180°C (360°F).

Depending on the weather and how hot your kitchen is, the dough may need another 30 minutes or so to prove. It should be visibly well risen to around double in size. Gently press a finger into the dough – if it leaves a little indentation, it's ready to bake; if it springs back quickly, it needs a little more time.

Place a small tin with 25 g (1 oz) of hot water at the bottom of your oven. This will create steam, which will help the dough to fully develop during the bake. Place the tins in the oven and bake for 12 minutes before turning them around, then bake for another 10 minutes. To check the bake, carefully turn one loaf out of its tin and tap the bottom. If it sounds hollow, it's done. If not, gently slide it back into the tin and return to the oven for a few more minutes.

Once baked, the cakes will be a lovely deep golden-brown colour over the top. Cool them in the tin for 5 minutes, then turn out onto a wire rack to cool completely.

Ginger fairings

Growing up in Cornwall, these intensely spiced biscuits were pure comfort for Michael, crunchy on the outside and chewy on the inside. They're super fragrant when baking, and the ginger is almost fiery on the tongue. They're a wonderful biscuit to make and an easy, tasty addition to your repertoire.

SEASONS ALTERED

If you like your biscuits more on the crunchy side, add a couple of minutes to the bake time. You could also push the bake even further and then crumble the biscuits to use as a topper on poached fruit served with thick cream. This is delicious beside the fire on a cold evening.

If you're unable to get golden syrup, use a good-quality, pure honey.

In summertime, fairings make a great ice-cream sandwich with vanilla ice cream!

Makes 10

110 g (4 oz) caster (superfine) sugar

220 g (8 oz) plain (all-purpose) flour

1½ teaspoons bicarbonate of soda (baking soda)

2 teaspoons baking powder

¼ teaspoon fine sea salt

3 teaspoons ground ginger

1½ teaspoons ground cinnamon

1½ teaspoons mixed spice

115 g (4 oz) unsalted butter, chilled and cut into 1 cm (½ in) dice

130 g (4½ oz) golden syrup or honey

Preheat the oven to 160°C (320°F). Line a large baking tray with baking paper.

Sift the caster sugar, flour, bicarbonate of soda, baking powder, salt and spices into a bowl. Add the butter and use your fingertips to rub it in until everything is well combined.

Add the golden syrup or honey and mix with a spoon until fully incorporated. (This dough can also be made in a stand mixer using the paddle attachment.) The mixture should be moist enough to roll easily in your hands.

Shape the mixture into balls approximately 60 g (2 oz) each, and flatten them slightly with the heel of your hand. (At this stage you can refrigerate or freeze them to bake later.)

Place the biscuits on the baking tray, spaced evenly apart and with room to expand during baking. Bake for 12 minutes, then rotate the tray and bake for another 4–6 minutes until they biscuits are spread flat and are golden all over.

Cool on a wire rack. These biscuits are exceptional still slightly warm from the oven, and even better with a cup of tea. Fairings will keep in an airtight container for up to 5 days.

Pictured on page 50 (left).

If you're keen to incorporate whole grains and diverse flours into your baking, this is the perfect way to do so.

Digestive biscuits were originally made in the 1830s with the aim of increasing dietary fibre to aid digestion – hence the name. These biscuits have a crisp texture, and can be made a little more indulgent by dipping them in chocolate. A much-loved biscuit in the UK, these are a daily constitutional taken with tea. Michael has been known to eat half a batch in one go. A spoonful of sugar, indeed!

This recipe was kindly shared with us by Dawn Woodward, founder of the wonderful Evelyn's Crackers in Toronto. A committed advocate of wholegrain baking, Dawn is a leader in the baking world, producing a huge range of exquisite bakes with a sense of place that celebrates the work of farmers local to her.

Oat flour can be made by blitzing rolled oats in your food processor at high speed, until you have a fine meal.

SEASONS ALTERED

Malt syrup isn't always easy to find. If necessary, you can successfully switch out the syrup sweetener in this recipe. Rice malt syrup is a fructose-free substitute that will work well and is widely available. These biscuits can also be made with maple syrup, the rounded maple flavour providing a delightful difference.

We are chocolate monsters in the James family, but the chocolate is, of course, optional. Without it, these biscuits are great with cheese – perfect as a snack or a light supper.

Makes 18

60 g (2 oz) honey
50 g (1¾ oz) malt syrup
90 g (3 oz) plain yoghurt
220 g (8 oz) wholemeal
(whole-wheat) flour
110 g (4 oz) oat flour
70 g (2½ oz) bran
3 g (¹⁄₁₀ oz/½ teaspoon)
bicarbonate of soda
(baking soda)
3 g (¹⁄₁₀ oz/½ teaspoon)
baking powder
10 g (¼ oz) fine sea salt
200 g (7 oz) unsalted butter,
chilled, cut into 1 cm (½ in) dice

For coating

200 g (7 oz) dark chocolate
(at least 60% cocoa)

Combine the honey, syrup and yoghurt in a small bowl and set aside.

Put the flours, bran, bicarbonate of soda, baking powder and salt in a medium bowl and whisk with a fork to combine and knock out any lumps. Add the butter and rub it in with your hands until you have a rough crumble with pea-sized lumps of butter still visible. Add the honey mixture and mix until the dough comes together. (This can also be made in a stand mixer fitted with the paddle attachment.)

Tip the dough out onto a dry benchtop and gently knead to bring it together. It should feel like a firm dough with only very slight stickiness. If it feels dry, you can add a little more yoghurt. Divide the dough into two pieces, shape each into a circle and roll it out until it's approximately 3 cm (1¼ in) thick. Wrap each disc in plastic wrap or beeswax and refrigerate for at least 1 hour, or preferably overnight.

When you're ready to bake, preheat the oven to 160°C (320°F). Line two large baking trays with baking paper.

Remove the dough from the fridge and place on a lightly floured bench. Using a rolling pin, roll the dough out to 5–6 mm (¼ in) thickness. Use a 7 cm (2¾ in) round cutter to cut out the biscuits. Don't discard the scraps – these can be rolled together and used to form more biscuits. Space the rounds out on your lined baking trays and prick the centre of each a few times with a fork.

Bake for 16–18 minutes, until lightly golden around the edges and slightly darker underneath. The biscuits should feel firm to touch, but not hard. Transfer to a wire rack to cool completely.

Once the biscuits are cool, temper the chocolate (page 17). Dip half of each biscuit in the chocolate and place them on a sheet of baking paper until the chocolate sets.

Store in an airtight container for up to 5 days.

Pictured on pages 50–1 (centre).

Brown butter sponge cake, with variations

There are so many uses for a great sponge cake. Perfect for afternoon tea, sandwiched with cream and jam, a sponge is also the base for such classics as lamingtons, Swiss rolls and kids' birthday cakes. There's a reason the Country Women's Association takes such pride in their sponges!

Browning the butter before you mix gives this sponge a lovely nutty, buttery quality. All the lift in this cake comes from the eggs, and the trick with this is to whisk them for at least 10 minutes on medium–high speed to create enormous aeration. Resist the urge to crank the mixer up to top speed – the air will hold better if it's built up over a longer period. Then gently sift the flour over the top and fold it in ever so carefully.

SEASONS ALTERED

Really, there's no season when a sponge cake isn't appropriate – they're so versatile. Michael grew up with a classic sponge with berries and cream, and to him it still tastes like home. Pippa's request every birthday was a passionfruit sponge. We've included both variations here.

This sponge is also a great foundation for lamingtons or trifle (page 174). You can use a 20 × 30 cm (8 × 12 in) rectangular tin and reduce the initial bake to 15 minutes before turning and baking for another 1–2 minutes as required.

Serves 8–10

60 g (2 oz) unsalted butter

4 eggs, at room temperature

125 g (4½ oz) raw caster
   (superfine) sugar

1 vanilla bean, seeds scraped
   (or 1 teaspoon vanilla paste)

125 g (4½ oz) plain
   (all-purpose) flour

¼ teaspoon fine sea salt

Preheat the oven to 160°C (320°F). Grease and line a 20 cm (8 in) round cake tin.

Put the butter in a small saucepan and melt it over a low heat. Leave it until it becomes foamy and starts to smell amazing, then set it aside to cool. If you have a few burnt bits, strain them out and discard. If you prefer a less toasty flavour, you can just melt the butter and take it off the heat before it starts to brown.

Whisk the eggs, sugar and vanilla in a stand mixer fitted with the whisk attachment on medium–high speed for around 10 minutes. The mixture should triple in volume and become pale and creamy.

In a separate bowl, mix the flour and salt with your fingers.

Sift a third of the flour mixture over the egg mixture, then use a spatula to gently fold it in, ensuring you scrape the side and bottom of the bowl to get an even mix. Repeat with half the remaining flour mixture, and then the last of it. Once the flour is almost mixed through, pour the butter over the top of the mixture and fold it in until just combined.

Pour the mixture into the prepared baking tin and gently even out the top with the spatula. Put it on the top shelf of the oven.

Bake for 20 minutes before checking. Turn the cake and bake for another 1–2 minutes as required.

Leave the cake to cool in the tin for 5 minutes before turning it out onto a wire rack to cool completely.

Passionfruit sponge

6 passionfruit

80 g (2¾ oz) icing
   (confectioners') sugar

200 g (7 oz) double (heavy) cream

20 g (¾ oz) caster (superfine) sugar

Halve the passionfruit and scoop the pulp and seeds into a bowl. You're aiming for around 120 g (4½ oz) of pulp.

Sift the icing sugar into a bowl and add roughly 1 tablespoon of the passionfruit. Mix thoroughly to create the icing. You want the mixture to be thin enough to spread, but not so runny that it won't set – it should be a runny custard consistency. Adjust by adding a little more passionfruit or icing sugar as required.

Whip the cream and caster sugar together to form soft peaks. When you lift the beater the cream should hold its shape, but be careful not to take it too far. Fold the remaining passionfruit into the cream.

Carefully cut the completely cooled cake in half horizontally. Place the bottom half on a plate and spoon the passionfruit cream on top. Use a palette knife to spread it evenly over the cake, right to the edges. Gently place the other half of the cake on top, then pour the icing over it. Use a clean knife to spread the icing all over the top, allowing a little to drizzle over the sides.

Raspberry ripple sponge

400 g (14 oz) fresh raspberries

70 g (2½ oz) raw caster (superfine) sugar

grated zest and juice of 1 lemon

200 g (7 oz) cream

200 g (7 oz) crème fraîche or sour cream (or make the mascarpone from the Tiramisu recipe on page 126)

1 vanilla bean, seeds scraped (or 1 teaspoon vanilla paste)

Combine 300 g (10½ oz) of the raspberries with 50 g (1¾ oz) of the sugar and the lemon zest and juice in a small saucepan. Place over a medium heat and bring it to a boil, then reduce to low and simmer for around 15 minutes until slightly thickened. Set it aside to cool completely, then add the remaining raspberries and mix them through.

In a separate bowl, whisk the cream and crème fraîche or sour cream with the remaining sugar and the vanilla until soft peaks form. Add two-thirds of the raspberry compote to the soft whipped cream and gently fold it through to create a ripple effect.

Carefully cut the completely cooled sponge in half horizontally. Place the bottom half on a plate and top with half of the raspberry ripple cream. Use a palette knife to spread it evenly over the cake, leaving a 1 cm (½ in) border around the edge. Dollop a few spoonfuls of the remaining raspberry compote over the top of the cream, leaving half for the top.

Place the other half of the cake on top and gently press it down so the filling just reaches the edge. Spread the remaining raspberry ripple cream evenly over the top and use a palette knife to create a wavy pattern. Dollop the remaining raspberry compote on top and serve.

Carrot cake

Is there anyone who doesn't have a favourite carrot cake that transports them back in time whenever they eat it? This ubiquitous classic is enjoyed far and wide, in many different and equally delicious iterations. The world has space for infinite variations of carrot cake.

This version has had the full James family treatment. Generously spiced, made with whole spelt flour and lots of carrots, this cake is a physically and emotionally nourishing expression of love.

SEASONS ALTERED

Why mess with a classic? As discussed, there are many worthy carrot cakes, so you do you. You could also add sultanas or currants for little bursts of sweetness.

Serves 8–10

4 eggs, at room temperature

250 g (9 oz) soft brown sugar

160 g (5½ oz) light olive oil

300 g (10½ oz) whole spelt flour

¾ teaspoon fine sea salt

2 teaspoons baking powder

1 teaspoon bicarbonate of
    soda (baking soda)

2 teaspoons ground cinnamon

1 teaspoon freshly grated nutmeg

400 g (14 oz) coarsely grated carrot

160 g (5½ oz) walnuts, lightly
    toasted and roughly chopped,
    plus 60 g (2 oz) walnut halves,
    for decorating

Cream cheese frosting

40 g (1½ oz) icing (confectioners')
    sugar, sifted

40 g (1½ oz) unsalted butter

1 vanilla bean, seeds scraped
    (or 1 teaspoon vanilla paste)

grated zest of 1 lemon

280 g (10 oz) cream cheese,
    softened

80 g (2¾ oz) double (heavy) cream

Preheat the oven to 180°C (360°F). Grease and line a 23 cm (9 in) round cake tin.

In a stand mixer, whisk the eggs and sugar for at least 10 minutes on a medium–high speed until light and fluffy. With the mixer still running, slowly add the oil as if you're making mayonnaise, until emulsified. The batter will thin slightly, so don't panic when it doesn't continue to thicken.

Sift the flour, salt, baking powder, bicarbonate of soda and spices into a large mixing bowl, to bring them all together and remove any lumps. The main objective here is to mix them well. The bran particles won't go through the sieve – don't discard them, just add them back in and mix well. Add the flour mixture to the egg mixture in three increments, folding gently between each addition until incorporated.

Add the carrot and walnuts in three batches, folding gently between each addition until incorporated. Use a spatula to scrape around the side and bottom of the bowl to ensure the walnut and carrot are evenly distributed through the mix, and don't sink to the bottom.

Pour the batter into your prepared tin and put it in the oven. Reduce the heat to 160°C (320°F) and bake for 50 minutes. Check and rotate in the oven and bake for another 5–10 minutes, or until the top is golden brown and a skewer inserted into the middle comes out clean. Cool in the tin for 5 minutes before turning the cake out onto a wire rack to cool completely.

While the cake cools, make the cream cheese frosting. In a stand mixer fitted with the paddle attachment, cream together the icing sugar, butter, vanilla and lemon zest until pale and smooth. Add the cream cheese a little at a time, continuing to mix at medium speed until smooth and creamy. Add the cream and mix just until combined – the mixture should be a spreadable consistency. Be careful not to overmix it, otherwise it will split.

When the cake has cooled, cut it in half horizontally and place the bottom half onto a serving plate. Spread it with half the cream cheese frosting, then replace the top. Spread the remaining frosting over the top of the cake and decorate with walnuts.

Black forest gateau with rye and buttermilk

'Are you making a BFG like the book?' asks Clover. No, kiddo, not a Big Friendly Giant, but a Beautiful, Fabulous Gala of a cake for special occasions, and for the love of cherries and chocolate.

Black forest gateau was Michael's preferred birthday cake as a child, and to this day it is still his favourite cake. It was also a fixture of Pippa's childhood – her mum would make the Margaret Fulton version. Pippa used to watch in fascination as the chocolate scrolls were magicked off the marble slab. This is our twist on the German classic, using rye flour and buttermilk in the sponge to complement the cherries and chocolate.

This is a big recipe, with many elements to prepare. Most of them are straightforward though, and can be prepared in advance to take the pressure off on the day. In fact, you can even assemble the cake the day before serving, and really take your time.

The chocolate bark resembles the forest floor, littered with fallen logs. Tempering the chocolate and making the scrolls takes time and care, but it feels like a miracle as the chocolate lifts and turns ahead of the knife. You will need small shavings of chocolate as well, so don't worry about making them perfect. Separate the successful scrolls from the shards as you go. Store the scrolls in the fridge, and put the shavings in the freezer until you're ready to assemble the cake. And be sure to save any excess chocolate for another use. The cake will keep for up to 5 days in an airtight container in the fridge. If keeping it over a few days, slice what you need and leave the slices out to come to room temperature before eating.

SEASONS ALTERED

This recipe calls for a cheat's jam to fill the cake, made with preserved morello (or sour) cherries. Preserved morellos are widely available, but if you are lucky enough to find fresh ones in season, definitely use those instead. You'll just need to cook them out for 15–20 minutes, to release the juices. Fresh cherries will give you a more vibrant flavour and a brighter colour. If you can find them in quantity, make a larger batch of the jam and store it in sterilised jars to use throughout the year.

Decorating the top of the cake with eating cherries gives a nice contrast, but outside of cherry season, preserved morellos will work perfectly well – just extract sixteen of the nicest looking cherries and set them aside before making your jam.

Serves 16

Cherry jam

1 × 400 g (14 oz) jar preserved
    sour cherries

120 g (4½ oz) caster
    (superfine) sugar

grated zest and juice of 1 lemon

50 g (1¾ oz) kirsch

1 tablespoon cornflour (cornstarch)

Cream cheese icing

550 g (1 lb 3 oz) cream cheese,
    at room temperature

280 g (10 oz) crème fraîche or sour
    cream (or make the mascarpone
    from the Tiramisu recipe on
    page 126)

140 g (5 oz) icing (confectioners')
    sugar

1 vanilla bean, seeds scraped
    (or 1 teaspoon vanilla paste)

Crème Chantilly

150 g (5½ oz) double (heavy) cream

20 g (¾ oz) raw caster
    (superfine) sugar

1 vanilla bean, seeds scraped
    (or 1 teaspoon vanilla paste)

Chocolate bark

200 g (7 oz) dark chocolate
    (at least 60% cocoa)

Chocolate sponge

8 eggs, at room temperature

200 g (7 oz) caster (superfine) sugar

80 g (2¾ oz) unsalted butter

150 g (5½ oz) plain
    (all-purpose) flour

50 g (1¾ oz) rye flour

60 g (2 oz) cocoa powder

10 g (¼ oz) baking powder

5 g (⅛ oz) bicarbonate of soda
    (baking soda)

¼ teaspoon fine sea salt

100 g (3½ oz) buttermilk

To assemble and garnish

16 fresh cherries

100 g (3½ oz) kirsch

To make the jam, pit the cherries and put them in a medium saucepan with the sugar, lemon zest and juice, and kirsch. Cook over a low heat for 5 minutes, until softened. Strain the juice into a small bowl and add the cornflour, stirring it in to make a cherry slurry. Return this to the saucepan and bring to the boil over a medium heat. Cook until quite thick, then add the cherries and stir to combine. Set aside to cool completely. The jam will keep refrigerated in an airtight container for a month.

To make the cream cheese icing, in a stand mixer fitted with the paddle attachment, beat the cream cheese on medium speed for a few minutes to create a smooth paste. Combine the crème fraîche or sour cream, sugar and vanilla in a medium bowl and whisk to soft peaks. Fold in the cream cheese and mix until well combined. Transfer into a piping bag and refrigerate until you're ready to assemble the cake.

To make the crème Chantilly, combine the cream, sugar and vanilla in a bowl and whisk until you have soft peaks. When you lift the whisk up, the cream should just hold its shape. Transfer to an airtight container and refrigerate until you're ready to assemble the cake.

For the chocolate bark, temper the chocolate and form scrolls and shards following the instructions on pages 17–18. Put the scrolls in an airtight container in the fridge and the shards in the freezer until needed.

To make the chocolate sponge, preheat the oven to 160°C (320°F). Grease and line two 20 cm (8 in) round cake tins.

In a stand mixer, whisk the eggs and sugar for about 10 minutes at medium–high speed, until pale and creamy. Melt the butter in a small saucepan over a medium heat, then remove from the heat and let cool.

Combine the flours, cocoa, baking powder, bicarbonate of soda and salt in a medium bowl. Gently transfer the egg mixture into a large mixing bowl and sift over a third of the dry mixture. Use a spatula to gently fold the dry mixture in, and then repeat twice more, until the dry ingredients are all incorporated. Combine the cooled melted butter with the buttermilk, then pour it into the batter. Gently fold the butter mixture in, then divide the batter equally between your two prepared tins.

Bake for 20 minutes, then rotate the tins and bake for another 6–8 minutes until a skewer inserted into the middle comes out clean and the surface has lost its eggy wobble. Cool on a wire rack.

To assemble your black forest gateau, cut each of the cakes in half horizontally. (If the tops are not even, you can trim them as well.) Place one piece on a plate and drizzle 20 g (¾ oz) of kirsch over the surface. Spread a third of the cherry jam evenly over the top then pipe a layer of cream cheese icing, piping just to the edges. Place another cake half on top and repeat this process with the kirsch, jam and cream cheese icing. Repeat with the third cake half, then place the last half on top and drizzle the remaining kirsch over the surface. Use a palette knife to spread the remaining cream cheese icing around the sides and over the top of the cake. You should now have a tall cake with all visible surfaces covered in cream cheese icing. Don't worry about making it perfect – the chocolate shavings will hide any slip-ups.

Remove the small pieces of shaved chocolate from the freezer and distribute them over the surface of the cake, gently pressing them into the cream to stick. If it's a warm day, you can put the cake in the fridge to cool for a while after this step, to prevent the chocolate from melting.

Retrieve your chocolate logs from the fridge and place them artfully on top of the cake to create your beautiful forest floor. Pipe the crème Chantilly in balls around the top edge of the cake, imagining the top of the cake as a clock face to space them evenly, until you have 16 dollops of cream bordering the circumference. Place a cherry on top of each one, pressing it in gently to make it stick. Return the cake to the fridge for at least 1 hour before serving.

Lemon poppy seed cake

This cake was extremely popular and in heavy rotation at Tivoli Road Bakery, but for some reason it didn't make it into our first book, *The Tivoli Road Baker*. Pippa often enjoyed a similar cake with her childhood friend Zoe, and is always delighted to be reminded of it.

The tiny poppy seeds provide a wonderful crunch. They're a rich source of dietary fats, and for this reason will go rancid quickly if you're not careful. Always keep them in an airtight container in the fridge or freezer, and avoid storing them for months on end.

We are so lucky to have access to Mount Zero's wonderful lemon-pressed extra-virgin olive oil. It's produced by pressing whole lemons with the olives, resulting in a vibrant, zingy oil which is great for cooking, both sweet and savoury. If you're in Australia, it's well worth seeking out.

SEASONS ALTERED

Hazelnut meal makes a good substitute for the almonds here. Finely chopped candied ginger in place of the poppy seeds creates a warming and aromatic bake.

Mount Zero also makes a yuzu-pressed extra virgin olive oil. The Japanese citrus fruit is so fragrant and distinctive; we've used it here with great success.

Serves 10–12

100 g (3½ oz) unsalted
    butter, softened
250 g (9 oz) raw caster
    (superfine) sugar
grated zest of 3 medium lemons
5 eggs, at room temperature
300 g (10½ oz) ground almonds
60 g (2 oz) poppy seeds
¼ teaspoon fine sea salt
100 g (3½ oz) lemon oil

Icing

110 g (4 oz) icing
    (confectioners') sugar
20 g (¾ oz) lemon juice

Preheat the oven to 160°C (320°F). Grease and line a 25 × 10 cm (10 × 4 in) tin.

In a stand mixer fitted with the paddle attachment, cream the butter, sugar and lemon zest for about 10 minutes, until the mixture becomes pale in colour and creamy in texture.

Lightly whisk the eggs in a medium bowl. With the mixer still running, add the eggs to the butter mixture in four increments, ensuring each is fully incorporated before adding the next. Stop and scrape down the side of the bowl as needed, to ensure everything is mixed well.

Combine the ground almonds, poppy seeds and salt in a bowl and mix with your fingers to work them together and remove any lumps. Add to the butter mixture and beat on a low–medium speed until well combined.

With the mixer still running, slowly add the lemon oil and beat for a couple of minutes until fully incorporated and well aerated.

Spoon the mixture into your prepared baking tin and bake for 45 minutes, then rotate the tin in the oven and bake for another 20 minutes until the cake has a deep golden colour over the top, and a skewer inserted into the middle comes out clean.

Cool in the tin for 10 minutes before turning the cake out onto a wire rack to cool completely.

To make the icing, sift the icing sugar into a bowl, then strain over the lemon juice and whisk to combine. Pour the icing immediately over the cake and use a knife to spread it to the edges, letting a little drizzle down the sides.

Brown poles

The National Gallery of Australia stands proud, lakeside under Canberra's big skies. A key piece in its collection is Jackson Pollock's *Blue poles*, a famously controversial acquisition by the gallery's first director, with the support of then Prime Minister Gough Whitlam. The conservative Australia of the day didn't appreciate the decision to spend US$2 million on an abstract artwork created by a foreigner, and the headlines were ruthless. Pippa stills remembers her first school trip to view the painting, and this important episode in Australian art history is etched in her psyche.

This simple yet decadent almond slice, topped with drizzled dark chocolate, is adapted from one that Pippa's mum used to make. She named it 'Brown poles', poking fun at the furore over the most talked about work of art in town.

SEASONS ALTERED

Try grinding dry roasted almonds into meal. The toasty flavour is wonderful with the sweet, toffee-like topping.

Makes 20 slices

Base

60 g (2 oz) unsalted butter, softened

110 g (4 oz) raw (demerara) sugar

125 g (4½ oz) almonds, freshly ground

2 eggs, at room temperature

30 g (1 oz) wholemeal (whole-wheat) flour

Topping

60 g (2 oz) unsalted butter

75 g (2¾ oz) caster (superfine) sugar

80 g (2¾ oz) honey

140 g (5 oz) flaked almonds

20 g (¾ oz) water

100 g (3½ oz) dark chocolate (at least 10% cocoa)

Preheat the oven to 190°C (375°F). Lightly grease and line a 20 × 30 cm (8 × 12 in) baking tray.

To make the base, cream together the butter and sugar in a stand mixer fitted with the paddle attachment, until pale. Add the almonds and mix until combined. With the mixer still running, add the eggs, one at a time, ensuring the first is fully incorporated before adding the second. Stop the mixer and scrape down the side of the bowl as required, to ensure the ingredients are well mixed. Add the flour and mix, then spread the mixture over the base of the baking tray. Bake for 10 minutes, until only just starting to colour at the edges, and then set aside to cool.

While the base is in the oven, make the almond topping. Combine the butter, sugar, honey, flaked almonds and water in a medium saucepan. Stir over a low heat without boiling, until the sugar is dissolved. Bring it up to a simmer and cook, uncovered and without stirring, for around 4–6 minutes, or until it starts to thicken.

When the base has cooled slightly, spread the topping over the base and bake for a further 10 minutes, until the almonds just start to colour. Allow to cool in the tin before transferring to a wire rack.

Once cool, melt the chocolate and use a spoon to drizzle it over the slice (channelling your inner Jackson Pollock!). Let the chocolate set and then cut the slice into rectangles 6 × 5 cm (2½ × 2 in).

This slice will keep at room temperature in an airtight container for up to 5 days.

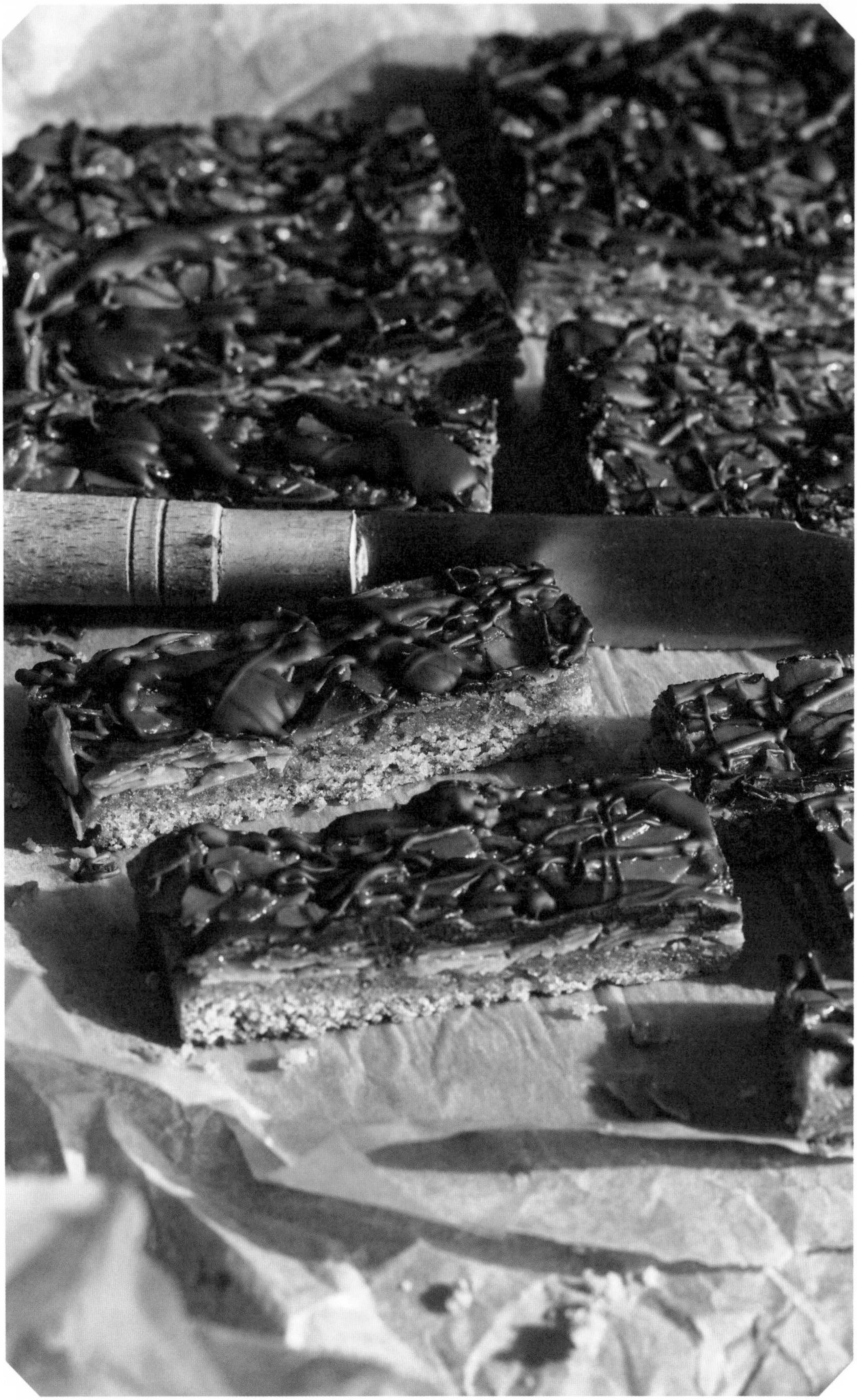

Feijoa mousse

Feijoas have an intensely floral perfume, a tangy sweetness and a slightly gritty texture. They are great eaten fresh, the inside scooped out and eaten with a spoon, and they also make a nice chutney. Growing up, Pippa's family had a prolific feijoa tree in the garden. Pippa's dad would make feijoa mousse every autumn in an attempt to use the glut. Stumbling upon a bag of feijoas at the farmers' market, we decided to explore that memory, and created this updated version. The white chocolate rounds out the flavour of the feijoa and acts as a setting agent.

A bit like avocados, a feijoa's moment of optimum eating is short-lived. Cut into a not-quite-ripe feijoa and it's astringent and sandy; leave it too long in the bowl and it's unpleasantly pungent.

SEASONS ALTERED

Any fruit that will puree could be used here – think mango, kiwi, even stewed rhubarb. Toasted macadamias provide textural contrast and are rich enough to hold the slight astringency of the feijoas. Almonds or hazelnuts would be good alternatives.

Serves 6

200 g (7 oz) feijoas

250 g (9 oz) double (heavy) cream

1 vanilla bean, seeds scraped
  (or 1 teaspoon vanilla paste)

4 egg yolks, at room temperature

90 g (3 oz) caster (superfine) sugar

80 g (2¾ oz) white chocolate

20 g (¾ oz) lemon juice
  (roughly half a lemon)

3 egg whites, at room temperature

100 g (3½ oz) macadamias,
  lightly toasted, to serve

Peel the feijoas and put the pulp into a food processor. Alternately pulse the machine and scrape down the side of the bowl until you have a smooth puree. You're aiming for around 150 g (5½ oz) of puree.

Heat the cream and vanilla in a saucepan over a medium heat and bring the mixture to a very light simmer, ensuring it doesn't boil. In a medium bowl, whisk together the egg yolks and 60 g (2 oz) of the sugar until slightly pale. Add the yolk mixture to the saucepan, whisking constantly to keep the eggs from scrambling. Continue to cook over a medium heat, stirring constantly, for about 5 minutes. Alternate between using a whisk and a spatula – the whisk brings everything together and removes any lumps as they appear; the spatula is used to scrape the side and base of the saucepan, to stop any spots catching. Cook until the mixture coats the back of a spoon.

Remove the saucepan from the heat and add the white chocolate, stirring until it's melted and incorporated fully. Add the feijoa pulp and mix well.

In a stand mixer, whisk the egg whites and the remaining 30 g (1 oz) sugar to firm peaks. Add a spoonful of this mixture to the feijoa custard and mix it in, then gently fold in the rest. Divide the mousse between six serving glasses or bowls and set in the fridge for at least 3 hours, or overnight.

Just before serving, roughly chop the toasted nuts, then sprinkle them over the top of each mousse for a lovely crunch.

Lemon posset

Sometimes you just want an easy and effective recipe, one that showcases outstanding produce and produces a result that belies the effort made. A zesty, not-too-sweet set cream, lemon posset ticks that box – with a slight disclaimer. When we lived in the UK we used to make this often. After returning to Australia, we found with dismay that our trusty recipe repeatedly failed. Most cream sold in Australian supermarkets contains thickening gums or gelatine to make up for a lack of fat in the cream, a result of different pastures here. The difference meant the heat and acid didn't produce the desired chemical reaction in the cream, and we ended up with a thin crust barely containing a liquid lemony centre.

We've tweaked the recipe and can now confirm it will work with Aussie cream. But we still recommend seeking out pure cream with a minimum fat content of 40%. Watch the temperature very carefully – you don't want the cream to boil over, and once you reduce the heat you need to hold a very gentle simmer, or it won't set.

SEASONS ALTERED

When fresh berries or figs aren't an option, finish with lightly toasted and roughly chopped pistachios or almonds.

Passionfruit posset is also fabulous. Passionfruit is less acidic than lemon, so add lime juice to aid the setting. 100 g (3½ oz) passionfruit pulp plus 30 g (1 oz) lime juice works well to replace the lemon.

Serves 4

500 g (1 lb 2 oz) double (heavy) cream

100 g (3½ oz) golden caster (superfine) sugar

120 g (4½ oz) lemon juice plus grated zest of 1 lemon

4 pieces Wholemeal shortbread (page 37), to serve

fresh berries or figs, to serve

Combine the cream and sugar in a heavy-based saucepan over a medium heat and bring the temperature up, stirring to dissolve the sugar. The cream will start to expand just before it comes to the boil; watch for that moment, then reduce the heat to low before it boils over. Simmer very gently on a low heat for 5 minutes, watching the pot to ensure it never boils.

Remove from the heat and stir through the lemon juice and zest. Divide the cream between four small cups or bowls and place in the fridge. Leave to set for 6 hours, or overnight.

To serve, scatter a few berries or figs over the top of each posset. These are best eaten with a teaspoon and a plate of Wholemeal shortbread (page 37) in the middle of the table, for your guests to help themselves to.

Warm rice pudding with berry compote

Our relationship with food is often a journey, and the story of this rice pudding is a good illustration of that.

Ambrosia rice pudding is a school dinner staple in the UK. Gluggy and sweet, for many grown adults rice pudding is a horrid reminder of their school days; for others, it's a visceral comfort. Michael quite liked the tinned stuff, but when he moved to London and worked at Pied à Terre, the two Michelin-starred restaurant then headed by chef Tom Aikens, he made this version. It was a revelation – so simple, but perfectly creamy and absolutely delicious (even though it was served with mango, freighted in from many miles away).

Fast forward twenty-five years, and we've long been thinking more deeply about the food we eat – where it comes from, how it's made and how it impacts us and others. While we're not eating air-freighted mangoes, this rice pudding recipe has stood the test of time. The key to a great rice pudding is time: cook it slowly and gently, stirring occasionally until you get that beautiful creamy consistency.

SEASONS ALTERED

Fresh fruit in season can replace the compote to perfectly complement your rice pudding.

Cornish strawberries, freshly picked at the start of summer, are a source of pride for the Cornish, and rightly so. Any fresh berry will work brilliantly here; the slight acidity will lift the richness of the pudding. Living in Melbourne, we are lucky to have a short season of Victorian-grown mangoes which are also perfect.

Throughout colder months, poached plums preserved in the summer finish a simple midweek dessert. Gently poached rhubarb is also wonderful. You could also forgo the fruit altogether, and simply grate some nutmeg over the pudding just before serving.

Serves 4

120 g (4½ oz) short grain rice
840 g (1 lb 14 oz) full-cream
　　(whole) milk
240 g (8½ oz) double (heavy) cream
60 g (2 oz) raw (demerara) sugar
1 vanilla bean, seeds scraped
　　(or 1 teaspoon vanilla paste)
grated zest of 1 lemon or orange
1 quantity Berry and rose geranium
　　compote (page 198)

Place all the ingredients except the compote into a saucepan and stir to combine. Bring to a gentle simmer over a medium heat, then reduce to low. Cook, uncovered, for 25–30 minutes, stirring occasionally, until the rice has absorbed most of the liquid. It should still be soft and creamy in texture, with some liquid still visible.

Divide the rice between four small bowls, top with the compote and serve.

Seasons
fast

Quick recipes for
hurried seasons

Pages 69–93

In a world of speed and information overload, we've become accustomed to instant gratification. This chapter is designed to give you (almost) that, from quick and easy cakes to our all-time favourite cookies. While we probably spend more of our time and income than most people on food, we are also in a time-poor season of life, and we want to eat well regardless.

As we move into busy middle life, with a school-aged child and too much to do, these are the recipes we reach for most often. We spend our Saturday mornings provisioning, and on Sundays we prepare for the week ahead, making it a little easier to reach for food that will sustain and energise us throughout the week.

The muesli bars are not even baked, and so quick to make. We've provided several variations, but often we just empty the pantry into the bowl. This is the ultimate adaptable recipe: use what you like and what you have. Muffins are another favourite to bake for the week ahead. Half an hour on a Sunday can save so much time on a weekday morning as you're scrambling to get out of the house. Perfect for the lunchbox or as a quick afternoon snack, these muffins are also great for breakfast. These recipes can be enjoyed throughout the seasons. Just use the base recipe and switch out the fillings with whatever is most abundant at the time.

Another way to save time in the kitchen is to batch your prep and bake as needed. Cookies are a wonderful prep-ahead bake, and we often have some made up in the freezer, ready to pull out and throw in the oven. There are a few styles here, from a light and delicate peanut butter cookie to the most decadent chocolate, rye and hazelnut brownie cookie. The choc chip and walnut cookie is made with wholemeal (whole-wheat) flour and packed with flavour. We make them often and never tire of them. No matter your mood, there's a cookie for you.

Baking ahead can also mean choosing something that will last the week on the bench. We have several different brownies to choose from, all of which are simple to make and will do just that. Wholesome cakes baked with nuts or wholegrains fit the same bill. Rather than going stale quickly, they'll improve over a couple of days and then hold up for several more. Many of the recipes in this chapter are made largely from pantry staples, ably supported by seasonal fruit or vegetables.

Perfect for your busiest season.

Muesli bars

The simplest lunchbox filler or bushwalking snack, muesli bars are great for their easy transportability, tasty snackability and calorie-dense nutrition. It's awful the way they've been coopted by Big Food, filled with refined sugar and stabilisers, wrapped in plastic and sold as a 'health food'. Still a sweet treat to be enjoyed in moderation, homemade muesli bars are much tastier and better for you.

SEASONS ALTERED

This recipe provides a base and some suggestions that work well, but as long as you have the proportion of wet to dry ingredients roughly right, you can use whatever you like here. Pippa will often make a variation of these on a Sunday night for school snacks. They're quick to prep, can be popped in the fridge and are ready to chop in the morning, ready for the lunchbox.

Makes 20 bars

Base recipe

120 g (4½ oz) rolled oats
120 g (4½ oz) pepitas
   (pumpkin seeds)
120 g (4½ oz) sunflower seeds
120 g (4½ oz) sesame seeds
45 g (1½ oz) chia seeds
150 g (5½ oz) unsalted butter
135 g (5 oz) honey
90 g (3 oz) caster (superfine) sugar
135 g (5 oz) tahini

Variations (add to dry mixture)

75 g (2¾ oz) each roughly
   chopped dried mango and
   flaked coconut
75 g (2¾ oz) each cacao nibs
   or chocolate chips and
   buckwheat groats
75 g (2¾ oz) each roughly
   chopped dried fig and barberries

Line a 20 × 30 cm (8 × 12 in) baking tin with baking paper, ensuring the ends of the paper extend just past the top of the tin – this provides the handles you need to get the bars out of the tin once set.

Combine all the dry ingredients in a large bowl and mix well so everything is evenly distributed.

Combine the butter, honey, sugar and tahini in a medium saucepan and cook over a medium heat. Use a whisk to combine the mixture as the butter and tahini melt, and continue whisking over the heat until the mixture thickens into a caramel and pulls away from the side of the saucepan.

Pour the caramel over the dry ingredients and mix with a spoon until all the dry ingredients are bound in the caramel. The caramel sets as it cools, so it may initially feel like you can't work the caramel through fully. Work quickly and persist – you'll get there!

Transfer the mixture to your tin and press it firmly into all corners. Work with wet hands to reduce the mess and spread the mixture evenly. Refrigerate for a couple of hours, or overnight, then remove from the tin and cut into bars. Store in an airtight container in the fridge for up to 1 week.

Often, we have many jars in the pantry, each containing a small amount of a baking ingredient such as nuts, seeds, different types of sugar, or the last of a sample of flour that we've been experimenting with. One day Pippa was pootling around the kitchen trying to think of something to bake as a lunchbox snack, and decided to pull out all the little jars and see what she could make. Half a jar of pepitas plus some bran, a bit of butternut pumpkin and the remains of a packet of cream cheese were reminiscent of pumpkin pie, and so this muffin was born.

SEASONS ALTERED

This recipe is ripe for alterations, so have a think about what works well together and use up what you have. Apple and almond, pear with roasted macadamias, beetroot with mixed nuts and seeds quickly toasted. Basically, you can use any nuts or seeds you like, or a mixture of several, roughly chopped. The butternut could be swapped out for anything slightly sweet that you can grate.

Makes 12 muffins

150 g (5½ oz) wholemeal (whole-wheat) flour

1 teaspoon baking powder

½ teaspoon bicarbonate of soda (baking soda)

¼ teaspoon fine sea salt

120 g (4½ oz) pepitas (pumpkin seeds)

30 g (1 oz) bran

1 teaspoon ground cinnamon

¼ teaspoon ground ginger

¼ teaspoon grated nutmeg

¼ teaspoon ground allspice

¼ teaspoon ground cloves

2 eggs, at room temperature

120 g (4½ oz) caster (superfine) sugar

230 g (8 oz) sunflower oil

240 g (8½ oz) butternut pumpkin (winter squash), grated

Cream cheese frosting

300 g (10½ oz) cream cheese

80 g (2¾ oz) maple syrup

1 teaspoon vanilla paste

Preheat the oven to 170°C (340°F). Line a 12-hole muffin tray.

In a medium bowl, combine the flour, baking powder, bicarbonate of soda and salt, and whisk with a fork to mix them through and knock out any lumps. Add the pepitas, bran and spices, and mix well.

In a stand mixer, whisk together the eggs and sugar on medium–high speed until pale and fluffy. With the mixer still running, slowly drizzle in the oil. Continue to mix until the oil is well incorporated.

Fold the flour mixture into the egg mixture, mixing until just combined. Add the grated pumpkin and gently fold it through. Spoon the mixture into your muffin tray and bake for 25–30 minutes. The muffins are ready when they're golden brown and a skewer inserted into the middle comes out clean.

Meanwhile, make the cream cheese frosting by combining the cream cheese, maple syrup and vanilla in a food processor. Mix until well combined and nice and smooth, with no lumps.

When the muffins are completely cool, spoon some of the frosting onto each one and spread it over the top. If you're keeping them over several days, store the muffins at room temperature in an airtight container, and keep the frosting in the fridge. Add the frosting just before eating.

Zucchini and marmalade muffins

Anyone with a veggie patch knows that you need several zucchini recipes in your back pocket. Once the summer warms up, they fruit prolifically. We love to eat ours raw, shredded with a zesty dressing, or grilled on the barbecue and dressed with soft herbs. Zucchini has a great texture for baking and works well with punchy flavours. We also find ourselves pickling jars and jars of it to use throughout the winter.

The marmalade in this muffin is the star of the show. The bittersweet flavour makes it a bit grown-up, and the walnuts give a nutty earthiness and texture. Marmalade seems to taste of the olden days, and is a match made in heaven with a nice cup of tea.

SEASONS ALTERED

You can use any type of squash for this recipe. In late autumn, carrots or a savoury variety of pumpkin would also work well. If you've been jamming berries, use the jam instead of marmalade, with a tart apple in place of the zucchini.

Makes 12 muffins

250 g (9 oz) wholemeal (whole-wheat) flour

1 teaspoon baking powder

½ teaspoon bicarbonate of soda (baking soda)

1 teaspoon cinnamon

¼ teaspoon fine sea salt

2 eggs, at room temperature

120 g (4½ oz) raw (demerara) sugar

240 g (8½ oz) Seville orange marmalade (page 207)

160 g (5½ oz) sunflower oil

280 g (10 oz) zucchini (courgette), grated

120 g (4½ oz) walnuts, roughly chopped

Candied mixed peel (page 215), to garnish (optional)

Preheat the oven to 170°C (340°F). Line a 12-hole muffin tray.

In a medium bowl, combine the flour, baking powder, bicarbonate of soda, cinnamon and salt. Whisk with a fork to mix them through and knock out any lumps.

In a stand mixer, whisk together the eggs, sugar and marmalade on medium–high speed until pale and fluffy. With the mixer still running, slowly drizzle in the oil. Continue to mix until the oil is well incorporated.

Add the flour mixture to the egg mixture and fold it through until just combined – you don't want to see any flour. Fold in the zucchini and walnuts. Spoon the mixture into your muffin tray and top with the candied peel, if using. Bake for 25–30 minutes. The muffins are ready when they're golden brown and a skewer inserted into the centre comes out clean.

Pictured on page 74 (right).

Chocolate, rye and hazelnut brownie cookies

Michael is the ultimate chocolate addict and a variation of this cookie has been in his repertoire for many years. From high-end restaurants in London to bakeries in Melbourne and beyond, this is one he keeps coming back to. It is a very grown-up cookie, with a fragile, cracked outer layer and a decadently rich, chocolatey centre. The rye flour gives an earthiness, and the hazelnuts provide that classic nutella-like vibe (but so much better).

SEASONS ALTERED

Australian native macadamias are an ideal substitute for hazelnuts. Pistachios are another beautiful alternative that marry well with chocolate. You can also add dried fruit such as sour cherries, barberries, or even apricots. It's hard to go wrong!

Makes 18

300 g (10½ oz) dark chocolate (at least 60% cocoa)

45 g (1½ oz) unsalted butter

3 eggs, at room temperature

225 g (8 oz) muscovado sugar

1 vanilla bean, seeds scraped (or 1 teaspoon vanilla paste)

40 g (1½ oz) rye flour

½ teaspoon fine sea salt

¾ teaspoon baking powder

150 g (5½ oz) milk chocolate chips

75 g (2¾ oz) toasted hazelnuts, roughly chopped

fine sea salt, for sprinkling

Melt the chocolate and butter together in a medium bowl over a pan of simmering water.

In a stand mixer, whisk the eggs, sugar and vanilla on medium–high speed for at least 10 minutes until pale, light and airy. Aeration is important to ensure your cookies have a lovely crackled top once baked.

Combine the flour, salt and baking powder, then use a spatula to fold gently into the egg mixture. Ensure the flour mixture is fully incorporated by turning the bowl and reaching down to the bottom as you fold.

Add the melted chocolate mixture and fold until just combined. Add the chocolate chips and hazelnuts, and mix until combined. Transfer the mixture to a covered container and refrigerate overnight, or until set.

When you're ready to bake your cookies, preheat the oven to 170°C (340°F) and line two baking trays with baking paper. Divide the dough into 60 g (2 oz) balls (at this point they can be frozen and baked when needed). Place the balls onto your lined trays, allowing plenty of space between them as they will spread during baking. Bake for 10–12 minutes. If baked from frozen, they may take an extra couple of minutes.

Once baked, sprinkle each cookie with a little sea salt and leave to cool on a wire rack. They will keep in a sealed container at room temperature for up to 5 days – if you are able to resist the temptation of eating them all at once!

Pictured on page 50 (right).

Peanut butter cookies

This cookie has been a long-time labour of love. The sought-after result has been elusive – light, crisp, full of peanut butter flavour but without the gluey texture that peanut butter sometimes gives. And this is it. These have more of a shortbread texture than a traditional American cookie, and they're very moreish. American bakers may know them as Nutter Butters.

You want good aeration in the dough to achieve a light cookie that spreads well during baking. Cream the butter and sugar for at least 10 minutes, and be gentle when folding in the oats and peanut butter to maintain that lightness in the dough.

SEASONS ALTERED

These cookies are sensational on their own, but a peanut butter cookie just about begs to be made into a sandwich. A swipe of strawberry or raspberry jam between two cookies makes the ultimate wicked snack.

Makes 15 cookies

175 g (6 oz) unsalted butter, softened

1 vanilla bean, seeds scraped (or 1 teaspoon vanilla paste)

65 g (2¼ oz) rolled oats

90 g (3 oz) raw caster (superfine) sugar

90 g (3 oz) soft brown sugar

135 g (5 oz) plain (all-purpose) flour

½ teaspoon bicarbonate of soda (baking soda)

¼ teaspoon fine sea salt

90 g (3 oz) chunky peanut butter (unsalted or lightly salted)

Melt 60 g (2 oz) of the butter in a small frying pan over a medium heat. If using vanilla bean, scrape the pulp and seeds into the butter as it melts. (If using vanilla extract, add it with the oats.) Add the oats and lightly toast them for 4–5 minutes, until light golden in colour. Once toasted, set the oats aside while you make the cookie dough.

In a stand mixer fitted with the paddle attachment, cream together the remaining butter with the sugars for 10 minutes on medium–high speed, until pale and creamy. Sift together the flour, bicarbonate of soda and salt, and then gently fold into the butter mixture. Fold in the oats, and finally the peanut butter, until just combined. Transfer the mixture to an airtight container, then refrigerate for at least 2 hours, or overnight.

When you're ready to bake your cookies, preheat the oven to 160°C (320°F). Line two baking trays with baking paper.

Portion the dough into pieces about 20 g (¾ oz) each – you should have 30 pieces in total. Roll each piece into a ball, then roll them back and forth on the bench, tapering one end to form a teardrop shape, with a slightly pointed end. Take two of these pieces and place them together with the points just touching. Using the palm of your hand, apply even pressure to flatten both pieces, so the adjacent ends join together, creating a peanut shape. Use a sharp knife to gently score a criss-cross pattern over the top, resembling peanut shell markings. Repeat with the remaining pieces, and place your prepared cookies onto the baking trays.

Bake for 12 minutes, then rotate the trays and bake for another 4–6 minutes, until the cookies are lightly golden. Set aside to cool on the tray. Once cool, these cookies will keep in an airtight container for up to 4 days.

Chocolate chip and walnut cookies

The combination of chocolate and walnuts is just so good. The use of wholemeal flour in this recipe complements the pairing and adds depth of flavour, resulting in a cookie that is the perfect balance of sweet, salty and nutty.

As this is a large batch of cookies, we often bake just half and freeze the other half once rolled. Having cookies in the freezer is like having a secret stash of loot. The dough keeps for up to 3 months in the freezer and can be baked from frozen – just add a couple of minutes to the bake time.

SEASONS ALTERED

Of course, you could use other nuts here. Brazil nuts, pecans or hazelnuts would all be great. For a different cookie altogether, white chocolate and macadamia are a fantastic combination.

Makes 18 cookies

220 g (8 oz) unsalted butter, softened

170 g (6 oz) soft brown sugar

130 g (4½ oz) raw caster (superfine) sugar

8 g (¼ oz) fine sea salt

1 vanilla bean, seeds scraped (or 1 teaspoon vanilla paste)

280 g (10 oz) wholemeal (whole-wheat) flour

5 g (⅛ oz) baking powder

3 g (⅒ oz) bicarbonate of soda (baking soda)

1 egg (60 g/2 oz), lightly beaten

350 g (12½ oz) dark chocolate (at least 60% cocoa), roughly chopped

175 g (6 oz) walnuts, roughly chopped

In a stand mixer fitted with the paddle attachment, cream together the butter, sugars, salt and vanilla. Start on a low speed and gradually increase the speed to high, until you have a pale and fluffy mixture. Scrape down the sides of the bowl as needed to mix everything well.

Sift the flour, baking powder and bicarbonate of soda together into a bowl. The bran particles won't go through the sieve – don't discard them, just add them back in and mix well.

With the mixer speed on low, add the egg in two or three additions. Run the mixer at high speed between each addition to fully incorporate the egg before adding more. Scrape down the side of the bowl as necessary.

With the mixer turned off, add the flour mixture. Mix at low speed until just incorporated.

Add the chocolate and walnuts, then mix at low speed until just incorporated.

Transfer your cookie dough into an airtight container and refrigerate overnight. This will help the flavours to mature, and your cookies will taste even better.

The next day, preheat the oven to 170°C (340°F). Divide the dough into 18 equal portions roughly 75 g (2¾ oz) each. Roll each portion into a ball, and then slightly squash each one into a puck. (At this stage you can freeze some or all of your cookies for future use.)

Line a baking tray with baking paper and put the cookie balls onto the tray, spacing them evenly apart. They will spread quite a lot during baking.

Bake for 14–16 minutes until golden and crisp. If you like them really crunchy, bake them a little longer. Cool on the tray for a few minutes, then enjoy a warm cookie!

Once cool, store in an airtight container for up to 5 days.

Miso caramel and tahini brownie

There are many ways to make a brownie. This one uses a different technique to achieve the required fudgy texture. The miso caramel introduces umami to the sweetness and, with a little sprinkle of salt, creates the perfect balance. The caramel encased in the brownie provides a delightful surprise in the eating, amplified by the occasional hit of tahini. Every mouthful is a taste sensation.

SEASONS ALTERED

This recipe will make more miso caramel than required, but there are other ways to use it. It's amazing drizzled over vanilla ice cream and sprinkled with toasted sesame seeds. Use it to sweeten up a banana and oat smoothie, or add it to a basic cookie dough. The caramel will keep in a jar in the fridge for weeks.

Serves 16

170 g (6 oz) wholemeal
    (whole-wheat) flour

½ teaspoon flaky sea salt

30 g (1 oz) cocoa powder

310 g (11 oz) dark chocolate
    (at least 60% cocoa)

220 g (8 oz) unsalted butter

190 g (6½ oz) caster (superfine)
    sugar

65 g (2¼ oz) soft brown sugar

1 vanilla bean, seeds scraped
    (or 1 teaspoon vanilla paste)

5 eggs, at room temperature,
    lightly beaten

50 g (1¾ oz) tahini

extra flaky sea salt, for sprinkling

Miso caramel

40 g (1½ oz) honey

200 g (7 oz) caster (superfine) sugar

60 g (2 oz) water

60 g (2 oz) unsalted butter

160 g (5½ oz) double
    (heavy) cream

60 g (2 oz) white miso

To make the miso caramel, combine the honey, sugar and water in a high-sided pan over a medium heat. Stir constantly to keep it a nice even colour, and keep an eye on it to avoid it colouring too quickly. When the mixture is a rich amber colour, add the butter and take the saucepan off the heat, continuing to stir until the butter is fully melted. Gradually add the cream, whisking well. Take care with this step – it will froth up. Whisk in the miso, then set the caramel aside to cool for a few hours, or overnight.

Preheat the oven to 170°C (340°F). Grease and line a 20 × 20 cm (8 × 8 in) baking tin.

Combine the flour, salt and cocoa powder in a bowl and whisk with a fork to combine and knock out any lumps.

Put the chocolate and butter in a medium bowl, and place it over a saucepan with a little water in it, ensuring the water doesn't touch the bowl. Melt over a medium heat, and mix to combine. Take the mixture off the heat and add the sugars and vanilla. Whisk until completely combined, then set aside to cool to room temperature.

Lightly beat the eggs in another bowl. Add half the egg to the chocolate mixture, and whisk until just combined. Add the remaining egg and stir until combined. Sprinkle the flour mixture over the top, and fold it in using a spatula, until only just combined.

Pour half of the brownie mixture into the tin, evening out the top. Pour about 250 g (9 oz) of the miso caramel over the brownie mix, spreading it evenly and leaving a 2 cm (¾ in) border around the edge – if it is spread right to the edge it will burn as it bakes. Dollop tahini over the top of the caramel, then scoop the rest of the brownie mixture over the top and around the sides to completely encase the caramel and tahini. Smooth the brownie mixture out evenly.

Bake for 15 minutes, then rotate the tray and bake for another 15–20 minutes. Test using a skewer – when the brownie is done, the skewer will come out with a few moist crumbs. Sprinkle with sea salt and leave to cool on a wire rack. The brownie can be stored in an airtight container for up to 5 days at room temperature.

Macadamia and raspberry blondie

Really good raspberries have to be one of the best fruits on Earth. Little bombs of bright acidity balanced with just enough sweetness, and a vibrant colour that's incredibly appetising. Their season is short enough to make the anticipation an annual mark on the calendar.

White chocolate is a useful ingredient to have in the cupboard. When used to sweeten and carry other flavours, it's a bit of a secret weapon.

SEASONS ALTERED

Rhubarb is an excellent substitute when raspberries are out of season. Just gently poach it in a not-too-sweet sugar syrup – you want the acidity of the rhubarb to meet the sweetness of the white chocolate. Pistachio and rhubarb are also a wonderful combination, so consider switching out the macadamias as well.

Serves 16

300 g (10½ oz) spelt flour

1½ teaspoons baking powder

1 teaspoon fine sea salt

2 tablespoons malted milk powder

200 g (7 oz) unsalted butter, softened

220 g (7 oz) dark brown sugar

2 eggs, at room temperature

2 vanilla beans, seeds scraped (or 2 teaspoons vanilla paste)

120 g (4½ oz) toasted macadamias, roughly chopped

100 g (3½ oz) white chocolate chips

100 g (3½ oz) raspberries

grated zest of 1 lemon

Roasted white chocolate ganache

350 g (12½ oz) white chocolate, chopped

200 g (7 oz) double (heavy) cream

Preheat the oven to 180°C (360°F). Grease and line a 20 × 20 cm (8 × 8 in) baking tin. Line a large baking tray with baking paper.

To make the ganache, scatter the white chocolate in an even layer over the lined baking tray. Bake for 5 minutes, stir, then spread in an even layer and bake for a further 5 minutes or until the chocolate is light golden. Stir again, then transfer the chocolate to a heatproof bowl. Place the cream in a small saucepan and bring to just below the boil, then pour the cream over the chocolate. Set aside for 1 minute, then stir until smooth. Set aside at room temperature until it becomes a thick, spreadable consistency.

Reduce the oven to 170°C (340°F).

Whisk the flour, baking powder, salt and malted milk powder together in a medium bowl to combine and knock out any lumps.

In a stand mixer fitted with the paddle attachment, beat the butter and brown sugar on medium speed for 10 minutes, until pale and light. Scrape the side of the bowl with a spatula, then add the eggs and vanilla and beat until just combined.

Add the flour mixture in two stages, beating at each addition until just combined, and scraping down the side of the bowl as required. Add the macadamias and white chocolate chips, and mix until just combined. The mixture will be thick. Transfer the mixture into your prepared tin and spread it out evenly with a spatula. Place the raspberries evenly over the top. Bake for 25–30 minutes until the blondie is golden on top, and a skewer inserted into the middle comes out clean. Transfer to a wire rack to cool.

Once cool, spread the ganache over the blondie, then cut into squares for serving. Store in an airtight container at room temperature for up to 5 days.

Crunchy buckwheat brownie

Buckwheat is the basis for many a gluten-free indulgence, and here is a wonderful example. It complements chocolate perfectly. Buckwheat is also a good cover crop that really should be more widely used for diversity in flavour and nutrition, as well as in the field.

The brownie we crave has a crisp, almost meringue-like top, and a gooey, fudgy centre. Some people love it plain, others want nuts. Here, the earthy flavour of the buckwheat provides a nutty undertone while the crispy groats bring little gifts of crunch with each bite. Start this recipe a day before you bake it.

SEASONS ALTERED

Use any neutral oil with a high smoke point to fry the buckwheat groats.

If you find buckwheat a little strong and pungent, you could use a different flour – rye or spelt will work well here. The texture could be provided by puffed quinoa or even popcorn. Cocoa nibs will give a decisive crunch and an extra layer of chocolate.

Serves 20

200 g (7 oz) buckwheat groats

500 g (1 lb 2 oz) sunflower oil, for frying

500 g (1 lb 2 oz) dark chocolate (at least 60% cocoa)

210 g (7 oz) unsalted butter

150 g (5½ oz) buckwheat flour

15 g (½ oz) cocoa powder

½ teaspoon fine sea salt

6 eggs, at room temperature

450 g (1 lb) soft brown sugar

1 vanilla bean or 1 teaspoon of vanilla paste

fine sea salt, to sprinkle

Start your crunchy buckwheat the day before you make the brownie. Cook the buckwheat groats in a saucepan of water until soft – basically, you want to overcook it. Drain and spread onto a tray lined with paper towel and leave to dry overnight.

The next day, heat the oil to 180°C (360°F) in a high-sided saucepan. Fry the buckwheat groats in batches for about 30 seconds or until light golden. Drain well onto paper towel and leave to cool.

Preheat the oven to 180°C (360°F). Grease and line a 33 × 23 cm (13 × 9 in) baking tray.

Melt the chocolate and butter together in a medium bowl over a pan of simmering water, then set aside.

Combine the buckwheat flour, cocoa powder and salt, and set aside.

In a stand mixer, whisk the eggs, brown sugar and vanilla for around 10 minutes until the mixture is pale, light and airy. Use a spatula to fold in the chocolate mixture in three batches. Be careful to fold very gently to avoid losing aeration in the egg mix. Fold until just combined, making sure you scrape the bottom of the bowl.

Sprinkle half of the dry ingredients over the surface of the egg and chocolate mixture, and use a spatula to gently fold them through. Repeat with the rest of the flour mix, mixing until just combined and ensuring you scrape the bottom of the bowl. The mixture should be quite runny. Gently fold in the crispy buckwheat groats until just combined, then pour the mixture into the baking tray and gently spread it evenly using the tip of the spatula.

Bake for 20 minutes, then rotate the tray and bake for another 8 minutes. The surface should be smooth and shiny with one or two cracks appearing. Cool in the tin for 30 minutes, then transfer the brownie to a wire rack and sprinkle the top with sea salt. The brownie should have a nice crispy top from good aeration and gentle mixing, and a gooey inside with pops of crunchy buckwheat. The brownie will keep for 5 days in an airtight container at room temperature.

Wholegrain apple cake

We like to have our cake and eat it too, so our favourite bakes are wholesome, expressive of the season and leave us feeling satisfied without a sugar rush. Pippa has spent several years tinkering with a recipe base that incorporates wholegrains and whatever fruit is to hand, and this is where it's landed. You can adjust this recipe by using different flours and different fruits – we've included some recommendations below.

SEASONS ALTERED

When we were given the remains of a bottle of rye barrel whiskey by our friend Topher Boehm of Wildflower Brewing and Blending in Sydney, we swapped out the brandy for the whiskey and used a mixture of rye and plain flour. The apple and rye were great together and the whiskey really sang. Perfect with lashings of freshly whipped cream.

A spelt and blackberry combination also works well. Use whatever sugar you have; brown sugar will give the cake a lovely richness and a softer texture.

Serves 8–10

2 medium sized apples

20 g (¾ oz) brandy

150 g (5½ oz) wholemeal (whole-wheat) flour

1 tablespoon baking powder

120 g (4½ oz) unsalted butter, softened

120 g (4½ oz) caster (superfine) sugar

3 eggs, at room temperature

Preheat the oven to 190°C (375°F). Grease and line a 20 cm (8 in) springform cake tin.

Cut the apples into 1 cm (½ in) dice, and combine in a bowl with the brandy. Stir the mixture thoroughly to ensure the liquid coats the apple, then set aside while you prepare the cake mixture.

In a medium bowl, combine the flour and baking powder. Whisk with a fork to mix them through and knock out any lumps.

In a stand mixer fitted with the paddle attachment, cream the butter and sugar until the mixture is pale and fluffy. With the mixer still running, add the eggs one at a time, ensuring each egg is fully incorporated before adding the next.

Fold the flour into the wet mixture, then gently fold through the soaked apple. Transfer the mixture to your cake tin and bake for 10 minutes, then reduce the temperature to 160°C (320°F) and bake for a further 40 minutes, or until a skewer inserted in the middle comes out clean.

Leave the cake to cool in the tin for 10 minutes before turning it out onto a wire rack to cool completely.

Serve with freshly whipped cream or crème fraîche.

One of the joys of choosing to eat local and seasonal foods is the anticipation of the next bounty, and every winter we wait for the stunning oranges that hit our farmers' markets. Sevilles for marmalade, sweet and juicy pink navels to eat after dinner, stunningly colourful and tart blood oranges for juicing and salads, and more. We are so lucky to have access to these fruits, and grateful to the farmers that bring them to market.

This cake is a simple way to introduce different flours to your baking, and a quick and easy way to celebrate when citrus comes into season. The slightly nutty flavours of the spelt complement the zesty orange exquisitely. This cake is perfect for afternoon tea, full of flavour but uncomplicated. It will leave you satisfied until dinner time.

SEASONS ALTERED

The gentle citrus notes in this cake are mostly from the zest. Take care to buy non-waxed fruit, ideally very fresh and in the peak of its season. The highly flavoured oils in the rind will fade with time, leaving the taste of the cake a little flat, if you use old fruit. It's also best to use flour that's as fresh as possible to gain maximum flavour and nutrition. Because this is a simple cake, it relies on the best ingredients, selected and handled with care.

Blood orange juice gives the icing a striking pink hue (pictured). Orange juice will create a subtler shade.

Serves 10–12

250 g (9 oz) unsalted butter, softened

250 g (9 oz) raw (demerara) sugar

4 eggs

grated zest of 3 oranges

100 g (3½ oz) plain (all-purpose) flour

150 g (5½ oz) spelt flour

1½ teaspoons baking powder

100 g (3½ oz) orange juice

80 g (2¾ oz) milk kefir

Icing (optional)

110 g (4 oz) icing (confectioners') sugar

20 g (¾ oz) orange or blood orange juice

Preheat the oven to 165°C (330°F). Grease and line a 25 × 10 cm (10 × 4 in) loaf tin.

In a stand mixer fitted with the paddle attachment, cream together the butter and sugar for around 10 minutes, until the mixture is pale and fluffy. In a separate bowl, whisk together the eggs and orange zest. Reduce the speed of the mixer and add the egg mixture in three or four increments, ensuring each addition is fully incorporated before adding the next. Scrape down the side of the bowl as needed to ensure everything is well mixed.

Combine the flours in a bowl with the baking powder and whisk with a fork to knock out any lumps. In another bowl, combine the orange juice and milk kefir, and mix well.

Add the flour mixture to the mixer bowl and mix on low speed until just incorporated. With the mixer still running, slowly pour in the liquids and mix until just combined.

Transfer the mixture to your prepared loaf tin and bake for 50 minutes. Rotate the tin in the oven and bake for another 10 minutes, or until a skewer inserted in the middle comes out clean. Cool the cake in the tin for 10 minutes before removing it, and then leave it to cool completely on a wire rack.

To make the icing, sift the icing sugar into a bowl and mix the juice through. You want the mixture to be thin enough to spread, but not so runny that it won't set – it should be a thick custard consistency. Adjust by adding a little more juice or icing sugar as required. Pour the icing over the top of the cake, spreading just to the edges and allowing it to drizzle down the sides. Let the icing set before slicing your cake.

Pistachio and cardamom cake

Pistachios are super tasty, vibrantly colourful and chock-full of healthy fats. In addition to being highly nutritious, they're also very forgiving to the baker – the high fat content provides incredible moisture and makes it *almost* impossible to overbake this cake.

We tend to use whole pistachios and grind them fresh, as they oxidise quickly once ground. A top tip is to freeze the pistachios prior to blitzing – they will hold their shape better and resist getting smooshed between the blades of your food processor.

Cardamom and orange zest add gentle lift and complexity, resulting in a simple yet elevated bake that's perfect for afternoon tea – preferably after a long, invigorating gardening session, or a walk in the great outdoors.

SEASONS ALTERED

Pistachio works wonderfully well with citrus. Try zesting three extra oranges or some lemon, and using this in place of the cardamom. This cake will also hold fruit in the mixture, so it's a good way to use up berries – raspberries or blackberries work particularly well.

Serves 10–12

For the cake

140 g (5 oz) unsalted butter, softened

250 g (9 oz) raw (demerara) sugar

1 vanilla bean, seeds scraped (or 1 teaspoon real vanilla paste)

grated zest of 1 orange

3 eggs, at room temperature

150 g (5½ oz) plain (all-purpose) flour

1 teaspoon baking powder

¼ teaspoon fine sea salt

150 g (5½ oz) pistachios, roughly ground

2 teaspoons ground cardamom seeds

140 g (5 oz) sour cream or crème fraîche

For the icing

110 g (4 oz) icing (confectioners') sugar)

20 g (¾ oz) lemon juice

To finish

30 g pistachios, roughly chopped

Preheat the oven to 160°C (320°F). Grease a 25 × 10 cm (10 × 4 in) loaf tin and line it with baking paper.

In a stand mixer fitted with the paddle attachment, beat the butter, sugar, vanilla and orange zest for about 10 minutes, until the mixture is pale and creamy. In a separate bowl, lightly beat the eggs. In several stages, add the eggs to the creamed butter mixture, mixing well between each addition to ensure the eggs are fully incorporated. Scrape down the side of the bowl as necessary to ensure the ingredients are thoroughly mixed.

Sift the flour, baking powder and salt together into a large mixing bowl. Add the ground pistachios and cardamom and mix well. Use a spatula to gently fold the flour mixture into the creamed butter mixture, in two or three batches. Finally, add the sour cream and gently fold it in until just incorporated.

Pour the mixture into your tin and use a spatula to gently smooth out the top, then bake for 40 minutes. Rotate the tin in the oven and bake for another 10 minutes, or until a skewer inserted into the middle comes out clean. Cool your cake in the tin for about 10 minutes before turning it out onto a cooling rack to cool completely.

Once cool, ice the cake. To make the icing, sift the icing sugar into a medium bowl and whisk in the lemon juice until the icing is a thick pouring consistency. Adjust by adding a little more juice or icing sugar as required. Spoon it over the cooled cake to cover the top, allowing a little to drizzle over the sides. Sprinkle the chopped pistachios over the top immediately, so they set into the icing as it cools.

Wholemeal chocolate cake

We are a chocolate cake loving family and this recipe is our go-to. It's a quick and simple cake for all occasions. First made for a last-minute dinner party, it's also perfect for a kids' birthday, or purely for the pleasure of enjoying cake on the weekend.

Don't worry too much about underbaking this one. You're aiming for a fudgy, almost brownie-like texture to the cake crumb. Once you get that risen, whole-cake-wobble then it's baked!

SEASONS ALTERED

This recipe was originally adapted from the famous Queen of Sheba cake, made with ground almonds. We have served that many times as a gluten-free chocolate cake and it's an absolute favourite. This one has a similar delicate crust – handle with care.

We've done a little more than simply swapping the nuts for grain, but you could make this cake gluten - free by reverting back to ground almonds, or using another nut meal in place of the wholemeal flour.

This cake makes a fantastic dessert with a little red fruit compote and fresh cream.

Serves 8–10

230 g (8 oz) dark chocolate
    (at least 60% cocoa)
220 g (8 oz) unsalted butter
½ teaspoon fine sea salt
30 g (1 oz) freshly brewed espresso
6 eggs, at room temperature
200 g (7 oz) raw caster (superfine)
    sugar
130 g (4½ oz) wholemeal
    (whole-wheat) flour

Preheat the oven to 160°C (320°F). Grease and line a 23 cm (9 in) round cake tin.

Put a medium saucepan with some water in it over a medium heat. Put the chocolate, butter, salt and espresso in a medium bowl and place it over the saucepan, ensuring that the water doesn't touch the bowl. Melt the chocolate and butter and mix well.

In a stand mixer, whisk the eggs and sugar on a medium–high speed for at least 10 minutes, until the mixture becomes light and creamy in colour.

Use a spatula to gently fold the melted chocolate mixture into the egg mixture, then very gently fold in the flour until just combined. Be careful not to overmix, or you will lose the air from the eggs.

Pour the mixture into the cake tin and put it on the top shelf of the oven. Bake for 30 minutes and then rotate and bake for another 8–10 minutes. There will be a few cracks on top, and when shaken gently there will be a slight wobble to the whole of the cake.

Cool on a wire rack for 1 hour before serving.

Seasons
savoured

Recipes to slow down to

_____

Pages 95–129

Even when we're not at work, we love to potter in the kitchen. For us, the ultimate luxury is taking the time to immerse ourselves in making something spectacular. Sometimes we're cooking to entertain, but sometimes we're simply following our curiosity, exploring a new technique or flavour combination, or a different way of using a favourite ingredient. We lean into the enjoyment of the process, and we always learn something.

So, this chapter takes a leisurely approach to some more involved or technical recipes. Some might take you out of your comfort zone, but stress should never be the main ingredient in your baking. Whether you're trying a new technique or compiling a dish of many elements created from scratch, taking it slowly will be far more enjoyable. Read the recipe in full, including the introduction and any notes. Check that you have all your ingredients. Break down the steps into smaller tasks so you don't get overwhelmed, and take frequent tea breaks. Your nervous system will thank you, and you'll get a better result to boot.

Working with choux pastry perfectly illustrates the idea that working with care pays dividends. Even with the most reliable recipe (and now you have one), you can end up with a stressful nightmare if you don't follow the details. Eclairs and profiteroles are sure to impress, and the French cruller is something a little different to try once you've nailed your choux.

On the subject of different doughs, develop your feel for yeasted brioche, a stepping stone to babka, bostock, Swedish cardamom buns and more. Babka, in particular, is having a moment, and everyone has a favourite. A staple of Jewish communities, babka is like a warm invitation to share in sacred cultural ritual. In fact, several of the bakes in this chapter provide a portal to different cultures, from the great bakes of France through to Portuguese tarts, Italian tiramisu and back 'home' for a very English baked custard tart.

Travel always sparks a desire to try new things, and we are fortunate to have met wonderful people in wonderful places, many of whom we now call friends. It's inspiring to see the way food is shared all over the world, and we love to translate some of what we've sampled when we're back at home. Of course, these days we can travel virtually, and through the many books on our shelves. We've also been inspired working alongside other bakers and at GrAiNZ gatherings. The food community shares generously.

By leaning into a slower pace, we honour and savour the produce we use, the cultures we're exploring and the people who have shared their recipes over many generations. What a gift!

Profiteroles make a beautifully delicate, few-bite delight, a treat offering wonderful combinations of texture and flavour. Quinces arrive at the market alongside the smell of roasting chestnuts, and the marriage of these flavours seems like the very expression of that time of year when the mornings are crisp and the leaves are turning.

Poached quinces, stored in sterilised jars, are a pantry staple that can be pulled out for many uses throughout the year. Chestnut cream can (and should) be made ahead to take the pressure off on the day of serving. You will end up with more chestnut puree than you need. There are many uses for this – one of the simplest is to enjoy it over ice cream, topped with shavings of dark chocolate. It can also be frozen for later use.

Create a guide for piping your choux by drawing circles, 4 cm (1½ in) in diameter, onto your baking paper. Turn the paper over and pipe onto the other side, using the drawn circles as your guide (page 35). The pastry is best baked the same day it's made, but if you're not using them all, profiteroles can be frozen once baked. Crisp them from frozen for 10 minutes at 180°C (360°F).

Makes about 20 profiteroles

1 quantity Choux dough (page 34)
1 quantity Poached quinces in
    syrup (page 211)

Chestnut puree

450 g (1 lb) chestnuts, in the shell
200 g (7 oz) caster
    (superfine) sugar
300 g (10½ oz) water
1 vanilla bean, seeds scraped
    (or 1 teaspoon vanilla paste)
pinch of fine sea salt

Chestnut cream

280 g (10 oz) double (heavy) cream
1 vanilla bean, seeds scraped
    (or 1 teaspoon vanilla paste)
250 g (9 oz) Chestnut puree
    (see above)

To make the chestnut puree, use a sharp knife to score a cross into the flat side of each chestnut. Put them in a large saucepan and cover with water. Bring to the boil over a medium–high heat, then reduce to a simmer for about 15 minutes. Remove the chestnuts one at a time, and remove the shell and pellicle (inner skin) while still warm.

Return the peeled chestnuts to the saucepan, and add the sugar and water. Bring to a simmer over a medium heat, then cook for 20–30 minutes, stirring occasionally, until the chestnuts are soft and the sugar is fully dissolved. Transfer to a food processor and add the vanilla, and some syrup to make into a smooth consistency. Set aside to cool completely.

To make the chestnut cream, whisk the cream and vanilla together until soft peaks form. Fold through the cooled chestnut puree and refrigerate until required.

Preheat the oven to 190°C (375°F). Line two baking trays with baking paper.

Put the choux dough in a piping bag fitted with a plain-edged 12 mm (½ in) nozzle. Pipe the dough onto the baking trays in circles roughly 4 cm (1½ in) in diameter and 2 cm (½ in) high, leaving a 5 cm (2 in) gap between each one. Don't worry if they're imperfect – use damp fingers to smooth out the surface and correct any misshapen ones.

Bake for 15 minutes, then rotate the trays and reduce the temperature to 180°C (360°F). Bake for another 15–18 minutes, until your profiteroles are a golden sandy colour all over. Set aside on a wire rack to cool completely.

Take a few pieces of poached quince and slice them very finely. You want the pieces to be similar in size to the baked profiteroles, but don't be too precious about the shape. Put the syrup in a small pan over a medium–high heat, and reduce it until you have a thick, fragrant syrup. Keep the syrup warm over a low heat as you fill your profiteroles.

Once cool, slice the profiteroles in half horizontally. Lay a thin slice of quince over the base of each one, and generously pipe chestnut cream over the top. Place the lid on top and gently press down so the cream spreads and meets the sides. Brush the top of each one with quince syrup, and serve. These are best consumed the day they are made.

SEASONS ALTERED

The classic profiterole is filled with a simple cream and glazed with chocolate, or engineered into the impressive celebration cake, the croquembouche.

We've also made this with apple and caramel. Whip some cream into soft peaks, and then fold through Apple sauce (page 214). Use this mixture to fill your profiterole, then top with a little caramel sauce and some toasted flaked almonds.

You can also purchase chestnut puree in jars or cans at specialty grocers. They contain varying amounts of sugar, and can also be quite starchy and firm. Loosen it with a little of the cream before whipping, and taste for sweetness. Add 100 g (3½ oz) of sugar to the remaining cream before whisking it with the vanilla and folding in the chestnut puree.

Lemon and raspberry eclairs with pine nut praline

Lemon, raspberry and pine nuts are so good together. The intense lemon yellow curd and pink frosting look amazing, too. You can make the praline ahead of time, as well as the raspberry puree for the glaze. The glaze itself should be made when you're ready to finish your eclairs.

Create a guide for piping your choux by drawing shapes 12 cm (4¾ in) long and 2 cm (¾ in) wide, with round edges, onto your baking paper (page 35). Ensure there's a 5 cm (2 in) gap between each one. Turn the paper over and pipe onto the other side, using the drawn shapes as your guide. The pastry should be baked the same day it's made, but if you're not using them all, eclairs can be frozen once baked. Crisp them from frozen for 10 minutes at 180°C (360°F).

SEASONS ALTERED

Any luscious cream filling can be used to make an eclair your own. Try filling them with Fig leaf custard (page 212) and then make a honey glaze to brush on the top, followed by a sprinkling of lightly toasted sesame seeds.

Makes 20

1 quantity Choux dough (page 34)
1 quantity Lemon curd (page 208)

Pine nut praline

100 g (3½ oz) pine nuts
220 g (8 oz) caster (superfine) sugar
120 g (4½ oz) water

Raspberry glaze

180 g (6½ oz) raspberries, either fresh or frozen
160 g (5½ oz) icing (confectioners') sugar

To make the pine nut praline, line a baking tray with baking paper and spread the pine nuts over the surface. Put the sugar and water in a medium saucepan over a medium heat. Heat, without stirring, shaking the pan occasionally to dissolve the sugar. Keep the saucepan over the heat until you have a golden caramel, and then carefully pour this over the pine nuts on the baking tray. Spread it out as evenly as possible and set aside to cool and set. Once completely cool, break into pieces and blitz it into a powder in your food processor (you could also use a mortar and pestle). Transfer to a clean, dry, airtight container and store in a cool dark place until required.

To make a raspberry puree for the raspberry glaze, blend the raspberries in a food processor, then pass the pulp through a fine sieve to remove the seeds. Place the remaining pulp in a small saucepan over a medium heat and reduce until you have around 40 g (1½ oz) of puree. Set aside to cool.

To make the eclairs, preheat the oven to 190°C (375°F). Line two baking trays with baking paper.

Put the choux dough in a piping bag with a plain-edged 12 mm (½ in) nozzle. Pipe it onto the baking trays in strips 12 cm (4¾ in) long and 2 cm (¾ in) wide, leaving a 5 cm (2 in) gap between each one. Don't worry if they're imperfect – use damp fingers to smooth out the surface and correct any misshapen ones.

Bake for 15 minutes, then rotate the trays and reduce the temperature to 180°C (360°F). Bake for another 15–18 minutes, until your eclairs are a golden sandy colour all over. Set aside on a wire rack and leave to cool completely.

To make the raspberry glaze, sift the icing sugar into a bowl and add most of the raspberry puree. Stir it in and check the consistency – you want it to be thin enough to spread but not so liquid that it won't set. Adjust the consistency by adding a little more raspberry puree or icing sugar as required.

Put the lemon curd into a piping bag with a fine-tipped nozzle. Use a skewer to make two small holes in the base of each eclair, just in from the ends and about 5 cm (2 in) apart. Take one eclair and gently insert the nozzle of the piping bag into one of the holes. Fill the eclair until it feels heavy. You should be able to fill it from one end until some of the curd squeezes out the hole at the other end. If it feels like it's blocked, place the tip of the nozzle in the second hole and try filling from the other end. Repeat for the remaining eclairs.

Dip the top of each eclair into the raspberry glaze, shaking gently to allow any excess to drop off, then place upright on a tray. Sprinkle with pine nut praline to finish. These are best served the day they are made.

French crullers

Choux pastry, but make it deep-fried. A French cruller is a little bit fancy, a little bit doughnut and a whole lot delicious. These are glorious when still warm from the fryer, and the cinnamon sugar is incredibly moreish. It's dangerously easy to over-indulge.

Makes 20

500 g (1 lb 2 oz) sunflower oil,
    for frying
1 quantity Choux dough (page 34)

Cinnamon sugar

100 g (3½ oz) caster
    (superfine) sugar
2 g (¹⁄₁₆ oz) ground cinnamon

Heat the oil in a large, deep saucepan or deep-fryer, to 180°C (360°F).

While the oil is heating, pipe out your crullers. Put the choux dough in a piping bag with a 10 mm (½ in) star nozzle. Cut out 20 pieces of baking paper roughly 12 cm (4¾ in) square. Pipe a ring of choux onto each piece of baking paper, about 10 cm (4 in) in diameter.

When the oil is hot, drop a ring of pastry, still on the paper, into the pan. Use tongs to carefully remove the paper, and fry the cruller on one side for 2 minutes. Gently flip it over and fry on the other side for 2 minutes, until deeply golden all over. Remove from the oil with the tongs and place it onto a plate lined with paper towel to absorb excess oil. Repeat with the remaining crullers.

Combine the sugar and cinnamon in a large bowl and mix well.

Once cool, toss your crullers in the cinnamon sugar to coat. Serve immediately. These are best when super fresh and should be eaten on the day they're fried.

SEASONS ALTERED

Cinnamon sugar is a universal favourite, but it's also a jumping off point. Use different spices to flavour your sugar – cardamom is wonderful, of course. Mix cinnamon, nutmeg, ground ginger, clove and allspice for a Yuletide cruller.

Serve with a rich hot chocolate for the ultimate fireside winter snack.

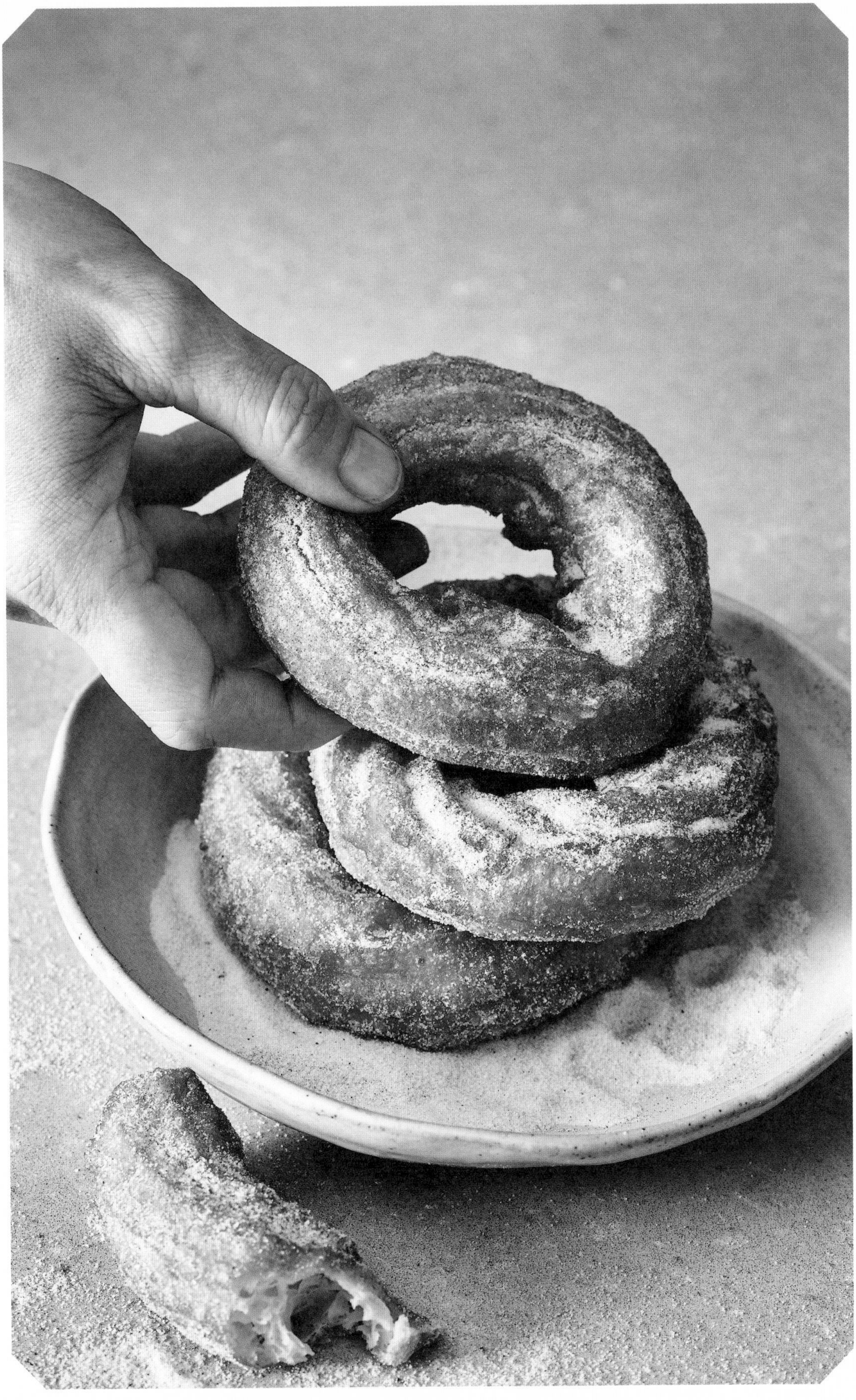

Cardamom palmiers

This is a wonderful opportunity to take on a bit of a technical challenge without having to concern yourself with dough proving temperatures and timing. It's a brilliant way to get into the world of laminated pastries, and ideal for a slow morning's work. Brew a pot of coffee and get the newspaper out to read between each step as the pastry rests. Palmiers can be made up in advance and baked at your convenience, and are great for snacks or morning tea.

Get a spray bottle filled with water and stick it in the fridge. Before laminating the sugar into the pastry, you'll apply a very fine film of water over the pastry so the sugar doesn't slide off when you fold or roll it. A pastry brush dipped in water and lightly applied will also work.

Cardamom seeds work best for this recipe. If you are using whole cardamom pods, use a mortar and pestle or a food processor, and sift or pick out the pieces of shell.

Use your sturdiest baking trays, the ones that will hold their shape in the heat of the oven. If the base is firm, you will get more even caramelisation and a crispy texture.

SEASONS ALTERED

Cardamom can be an acquired taste, so if it's not your jam don't let that stop you. Try cinnamon, anise, ginger, nutmeg or a combination of warming spices. Try orange zest combined with poppy seeds, or vanilla powder. Once you have the technique down pat, you are limited only by your imagination.

Makes 8

1 quantity Puff pastry (page 30)

Cardamom sugar mix

10 g (¼ oz) ground cardamom seeds
125 g (4½ oz) caster
    (superfine) sugar
100 g (3½ oz) soft brown sugar
150 g (5½ oz) raw (demerara) sugar
¼ teaspoon fine sea salt

To make the cardamom sugar mix, combine all the ingredients in a bowl and toss to mix well.

Roll out the puff pastry into a rectangle 12 × 24 cm (4¾ × 9½ in) and 1 cm (½ in) thick, with the long edge parallel to the edge of the bench. Lightly spray some cold water over the surface of the pastry, being careful not to use too much – your aim is to make the sugar stick, not to soak the dough. Sprinkle a thin layer of the sugar mixture over the surface, ensuring it is evenly covered.

Starting from the right–hand side of the rectangle, fold one-third of the pastry into the middle, then the other third over the top of that, as if folding a letter. Wrap your pastry and refrigerate for 1 hour.

Roll the pastry out into a rectangle roughly 20 × 48 cm (8 × 19 in), and 7 mm (⅜ in) thick. Position it on the bench so the short edge is towards you.

Lightly spray some cold water over the pastry, then generously sprinkle with the sugar mix, ensuring that the entire surface is covered evenly. Make notches in the edge of the pastry 23.5 cm (9¼ in) and 24.5 cm (9¾ in) from the bottom edge. Fold the top and bottom edges in to meet these notches. You will be left with a 1 cm (½ in) gap in the middle.

Spray the newly exposed surfaces of dough with water, then generously cover with the sugar mix. Fold the top half down over the bottom, using the 1 cm (½ in) gap as a hinge.

Spray the newly exposed surfaces of dough with water, and generously cover the surface with the sugar mix. Carefully flip the dough over and repeat so that both sides of the pastry block are covered with sugar. You should have roughly 50 g (1¾ oz) of sugar mix left after this.

Cut 2.5 cm (1 in) slices through the cross-section of the pastry so that each slice is held together by the hinged edge. Keeping the sliced block together, gently transfer it onto a tray lined with baking paper. Wrap the tray and place in the fridge or freezer overnight. The palmiers will last in the freezer for up to 1 month.

To bake your palmiers, preheat the oven to 190°C (375°F) and line two trays with baking paper. Remove the palmiers from the fridge or freezer, separate each slice from the block, and lay them out on the bench cut-side up.

Sprinkle the remaining sugar mix over the top and then turn them upside down onto the lined trays, leaving a 5 cm (2 in) gap between each one. Bake in the oven for 20–25 minutes (adding a few minutes if baking from frozen), until they are a deep golden colour and the pastry has expanded considerably. Remove from the oven and leave to cool on the trays for 10 minutes. Once the caramel has set, turn the palmiers over and break off any excess bits of sugar, then place on a wire rack to cool completely before serving.

Cardamom buns

These spiced, enriched yeasted buns are typically Swedish, although similar variations are popular throughout Scandinavia. They're currently having a moment all over the world, with many bakeries offering their version to their adoring customers. This one has a lovely hint of orange from the zest in the filling.

SEASONS ALTERED

Cardamom is a distinctive, highly aromatic and strongly flavoured spice. It's the kind of thing that immediately transports you to the place and time you first tried it. If you'd prefer a gentler quality to your buns, use ground cinnamon instead.

Makes 10 buns

Dough

8 g (¼ oz) black cardamom seeds, coarsely cracked

240 g (8½ oz) full-cream (whole) milk

400 g (14 oz) bakers (strong) flour

70 g (2½ oz) caster (superfine) sugar

6 g (⅕ oz) fine sea salt

8 g (¼ oz) instant dried yeast

1 egg, at room temperature

80 g (2¾ oz) unsalted butter, softened

Filling

120 g (4½ oz) soft brown sugar

110 g (4 oz) unsalted butter, softened

1 teaspoon black cardamom seeds, coarsely cracked

10 g (¼ oz) honey

grated zest of 2 oranges

Cardamom sugar

40 g (1½ oz) caster (superfine) sugar

40 g (1½ oz) raw (demerara) sugar

1 tablespoon black cardamom seeds, coarsely cracked

To make the cardamom sugar, combine all the ingredients in a bowl and mix well. Set aside until needed.

To make the filling, place all the ingredients in a stand mixer fitted with the paddle attachment. Beat until combined, then set aside until you're ready to use it.

To make the dough, first grind the cardamom seeds to a fine powder. Put the milk in a small saucepan over a medium heat. Bring the milk up to a gentle simmer – use a thermometer for accuracy, and remove from the heat when it reaches 82°C (180°F). Simmering the milk is not strictly necessary, but it changes the protein structure, resulting in a lighter, fluffier crumb once baked. Set aside to cool to room temperature.

Combine the flour, sugar, salt and dried yeast in the bowl of a stand mixer fitted with the dough hook. Add the milk and egg, and mix on medium speed for about 10 minutes, until the mixture forms a dough that stretches without tearing. Add the softened butter in two or three increments, then turn the speed to fast for 3–4 minutes until the dough comes together in a ball. Add the cardamom seeds and mix until incorporated. Turn the dough out onto a lightly floured bench, knead it for 1 minute and then shape it into a round ball. Leave for 30 minutes in a bowl covered with a clean, damp tea towel (dish towel). Place it on your bench and knead it for 30 seconds before returning it to the bowl and covering once more with the tea towel. Rest it in the fridge for 2–3 hours to cool.

When you're ready to shape the buns, take the dough out of the fridge and roll it into a square 30 × 30 cm (12 × 12 in). Spread the filling over the top two-thirds of the square, and then fold the bottom third up and the top third down (like a letter fold) to enclose the filling completely. You will have a rectangle that's 30 cm (12 in) wide and 10 cm (4 in) high, with two layers of filling running through it. Place it on a tray, cover with a damp tea towel and rest in the fridge for 10 minutes.

Make the egg wash by lightly whisking the egg, milk and salt together. Line two baking trays with baking paper.

Take the dough from the fridge and place it on your lightly floured bench. Roll it away from you until it's 25 cm (10 in) wide, 35 cm (13¾ in) high, and 8–10 mm (⅜–½ in) thick. Cut 10 strips vertically, 2.5 cm (1 in) wide. Roll each strip into a spiral and place into a greased muffin tin, or follow the more traditional method as follows.

Hold a strip of dough at one end, between your thumb and middle finger. With your other hand, stretch it gently and bring the other end towards you, looping it up and over your index finger. Loop it around once more, and then on the third loop, stop a quarter of the way around when you get to your thumb. Take your thumb out and press it gently into the dough to secure the loops, then wrap the remainder perpendicular around the first loops. Insert the end into the gap where your fingers were. You should have a loopy knotted shape. Repeat with the remaining strips.

Place the buns onto your lined baking trays, leaving plenty of space between them to expand. Cover the trays loosely with plastic wrap

Egg wash

1 egg
splash of full-cream (whole) milk
pinch of fine sea salt

Glaze

50 g (1¾ oz) Apricot and amaretto
jam (page 204)
50 g (1¾ oz) Seville orange
marmalade (page 207)
25 g (1 oz) water

for 1½–2 hours, until risen. After 1 hour, preheat the oven to 200°C (390°F) and place a roasting tin in the bottom of the oven.

Once risen, lightly brush each bun with egg wash and sprinkle with a good mound of the cardamom sugar. Carefully pour boiling water into the roasting tin in the oven to generate steam while baking. Lower the oven temperature to 180°C (360°F) and bake for 8 minutes, then turn the trays and bake for another 2–3 minutes until golden brown.

While the buns are baking, make the glaze. Place all the ingredients in a small saucepan over a low heat and simmer gently for 5–10 minutes, stirring occasionally to dissolve the sugar. Keep warm.

Once removed from the oven, lightly brush each bun with the glaze while they're still hot. Store at room temperature in an airtight container for up to 4 days.

Portuguese tarts

One of the original viral pastries, *Pasteis de Belém* are popular the world over. A combination of simple ingredients and technique, a great Portuguese tart is a beautiful thing. They're a bake that pastry chefs work hard to master.

The original Portuguese tarts were created at the Hieronymites Monastery in the area of Belém, which happened to be situated next to a sugar refinery. Following the Liberal Revolution in the early 19th century, monasteries throughout Portugal were shut down and the monks needed income. They started selling their tarts ... and the rest is history.

The tarts are baked in raw pastry at a very high temperature, resulting in a flaky and crisp golden base and a filling with a lovely singe on top. The flour in the custard helps to stabilise it, preventing your eggs from scrambling. The differences between a good tart and a great tart are getting the thickness of the pastry and the heat in your oven right. As always, when using simple ingredients, you'll get the best results when you use the best you can find.

Prepare the pastry and make the custard the day before you bake. You will need individual tart moulds to bake your Portuguese tarts. Moulds 7 cm (2¾ in) in diameter and 2 cm (¾ in) deep are ideal, but slight variations on this will be fine.

SEASONS ALTERED

These tarts will also work well with Flaky pastry (page 26).

Makes 18 tarts

350 g (12½ oz) Puff pastry
(page 30)
Apricot and amaretto jam, for
glazing (page 204)

Custard filling

200 g (7 oz) caster (superfine) sugar
150 g (5½ oz) water
500 g (1 lb 2 oz) full-cream
(whole) milk
1 cinnamon stick
1 lemon, zest peeled in strips
and pith removed
30 g (1 oz) plain (all-purpose) flour
100 g (3½ oz) egg yolks
(approximately 6 yolks)

On a lightly floured benchtop, roll out the pastry into a rectangle 25 × 40 cm (10 × 15¾ in) and 3 mm (⅛ in) thick, with the long edge parallel to the bench. Starting from the top of the sheet, roll the pastry towards you into a tightly rolled log. Wrap and refrigerate.

Make a sugar syrup by combining the sugar and water in a heavy-based saucepan. Bring to a boil over a medium–high heat, stirring to dissolve the sugar. Use a thermometer to monitor the temperature, and when it reaches 105°C (220°F) remove it from the heat and set aside to cool.

Put 400 g (14 oz) of the milk into a medium saucepan with the cinnamon stick and lemon peel. Bring to a simmer over a medium heat. In a medium bowl, whisk the remaining 100 g (3½ oz) of milk with the flour until smooth. Pour the cinnamon-infused milk into the bowl and whisk everything together, then pour it back into the saucepan and continue whisking over the heat until it thickens.

Remove the custard from the heat and add the sugar syrup in a steady stream, whisking continuously. Leave to cool to room temperature and then strain the mixture through a sieve. Add the egg yolks and whisk them in, then cover the surface to prevent a skin forming and refrigerate overnight.

To assemble the tarts, lightly grease 18 pastry moulds and place them on a baking tray. Remove your pastry log from the fridge and carefully slice it into slivers weighing 15–16 g (½ oz) each. Place onto the bench and roll out each one so that it's 1–2 mm (1/16 in) thick and then lay it over a mould. Use your fingers to gently press the pastry into the mould, leaving a 2–3 mm (1/16–⅛ in) overhang that sticks up around the edges. Once all your moulds are lined, place them on a tray and put them in the fridge for at least 1 hour.

When you're ready to bake the tarts, preheat the oven to 240°C (465°F). Give the custard mixture a little whisk, then pour about 40 g (1½ oz) of custard into each tart shell. You want each one to be almost full, with the custard sitting 2 mm (1/16 in) below the top.

Put the tray on the top shelf of the oven and bake for 10 minutes. Rotate the tray and bake for another 2–3 minutes, until the pastry is golden and the custard has dark scorch marks over the top. Leave to cool for a few minutes before de-moulding. Warm up a little apricot jam and glaze the tarts before serving.

Apple tarte tatin

This is an autumn warmer for that special time when the trees are laden with pome fruits. There's much excitement in the James home when the season starts to shift, and we wait with anticipation for the first bite of a perfectly crisp, tart-sweet apple when we've had our summer's fill of figs and stone fruit. It's also a great time of year to try your hand at making puff pastry at home, as the temperatures cool and your butter is less likely to melt as you work.

Once you've made your pastry and prepared your fruit, you can assemble the tarte and refrigerate until you're ready to bake. This makes it ideal for entertaining – just put it in the oven while you're eating the main course and impress your guests with the unbeatable combination of freshly baked flaky puff pastry, decadent caramel sauce and seasonal fruits.

Use a tart eating apple such as Braeburn or Granny Smith. We have a 24 cm (9½ in) cast iron tarte tatin pan, which is perfect for this recipe. You could also use a cast iron or heavy bottomed frying pan that will go in the oven.

SEASONS ALTERED

Apple tarte tatin is such a classic, but you can also use this technique with pear, poached quince (page 210) or any other fruit that will hold up to a long bake under pastry and will caramelise well. You also want to be sure the fruit won't release too much juice, which will make the pastry soggy. If you want something completely different and a little exotic, pineapple and star anise is a killer tatin combo.

Serves 4–6

300 g (10½ oz) Puff pastry
   (see page 30)
5 medium-sized apples, roughly
   800 g (1 lb 12 oz)
100 g (3½ oz) raw caster
   (superfine) sugar
60 g (2 oz) butter
1 vanilla bean, seeds scraped
   (or 1 teaspoon vanilla paste)
splash of apple brandy or
   lemon juice

Egg wash

1 egg
splash of full-cream (whole) milk
pinch of fine sea salt

Roll the pastry out into a disc 4 mm (¼ in) thick and cut a circle 1 cm (½ in) bigger in diameter than your tarte tatin pan. Place the pastry between two sheets of baking paper and refrigerate until you're ready to assemble the tarte.

Peel and core your apples, then cut them in half along the core.

Heat your tarte tatin pan over a medium–high heat. Add the sugar and allow it to melt a little, then add the butter to melt. Go gently adding the butter, as the heat may make it sizzle and splash. Cook until the caramel is a lovely amber gold, and then place the apples in the pan, cut side up. Add the vanilla and the apple brandy or lemon juice. Gently shake the pan and use a spoon to coat the apple well in the caramel, then set it aside to cool. Make the egg wash by lightly whisking the egg, milk and salt together.

When the filling is completely cool, lay the pastry sheet over the top. Tuck the edges of the pastry down between the apples and the side of the dish. Lightly brush the top of the pastry with egg wash and make a couple of steam holes. Refrigerate for 30 minutes to set the pastry, or until ready to bake.

Before baking your tarte, preheat the oven to 190°C (375°F). Bake for 25 minutes and then rotate the pan. Reduce the heat to 180°C (360°F) and bake for another 15 minutes, until the pastry is deep golden and puffed and flaky on top. Leave to rest for 10 minutes before inverting it onto your serving dish. Be careful not to burn yourself on the caramel! Serve with vanilla ice cream, Fig leaf custard (page 212) or cream.

It would be a hard heart that wouldn't melt for babka still warm from the oven. This dough is enriched with milk, eggs and butter, and creates irresistible aromas during the bake that will fill your home and bring the neighbours knocking. Originating in Jewish communities in Poland and Ukraine, this bake has spread widely with the diaspora. Jewish communities the world over connect with and express their identity through food, and babka is a celebrated part of that. We are so lucky to be able to share in this tradition.

Being an enriched dough, your babka will last for days and will also make an excellent house gift. It eats well when still warm from the oven, but the texture will hold up and the fat will carry the flavour. Be sure to use excellent quality dark chocolate and cocoa powder.

While this might look like a long recipe, there's less than an hour of actual work here. The rest of the time is in chilling, proofing and baking, requiring no hands-on action from you. You can bake it into a twisted loaf, in smaller pieces in a muffin tin, or even freeform on a baking tray if you have no tins.

The dough hydration may vary with the quality and moisture content of the flour, and time and temperature will vary from oven to oven. Trust your instincts here. And embrace the mess when twisting the dough. It's a sticky process but don't worry, after it's baked even the messiest babka will still look beautiful, and most importantly, will taste great.

SEASONS ALTERED

A dough spiced with cinnamon and studded with nuts or fruit makes a great alternative to chocolate. You can also create textural contrast by topping your loaf with hazelnuts or sesame seeds.

Makes 2 loaves

500 g (1 lb 2 oz) bakers (strong) flour
60 g (2 oz) soft brown sugar
315 g (11 oz) full-cream (whole) milk
1 egg
7 g (¼ oz) instant dried yeast
8 g (¼ oz) fine sea salt
80 g (2¾ oz) chopped
    unsalted butter

Chocolate ganache filling

40 g (1½ oz) cocoa powder
120 g (4½ oz) raw (demerara) sugar
1 teaspoon vanilla paste
150 g (5½ oz) double (heavy) cream
75 g (2¾ oz) unsalted butter, diced

Syrup

50 g (1¾ oz) water
50 g (1¾ oz) raw sugar

To assemble

100 g (3½ oz) dark chocolate pieces

To make the dough, combine the flour, sugar, milk, egg, dried yeast and salt in the bowl of a stand mixer fitted with the dough hook. Mix on low speed for 5 minutes. Scrape down the side of the bowl and use your hands to bring the dough together, ensuring you reach the bottom of the bowl. Check to see if it is too dry or too wet at this stage; it should be slightly sticky to touch.

Mix for another 5 minutes on medium speed. With the mixer still running, add the butter in two to three stages so it distributes evenly, and mix for 5 minutes until you have a smooth, shiny dough that stretches. Use the window pane test to check the dough: take a small ball of dough and gently stretch it between your hands – you should be able to stretch it very thin without it breaking. If you find that it breaks easily, mix for a few more minutes to continue working the gluten in the flour, then test it again.

Cover the dough with a damp tea towel (dish towel) and rest at room temperature for 45 minutes. Knead the dough on the bench for 1 minute and then return it to the bowl and cover with a damp tea towel again. Refrigerate for at least 2 hours, and up to 12. The dough will slowly ferment as it cools, making it easier to work with.

To make the filling, combine the cocoa powder, sugar, vanilla and cream in a medium saucepan. Heat over a low heat, whisking, until well mixed and just under a simmer. Remove from the heat, add the diced butter and whisk to combine. The mixture should be smooth and shiny. Refrigerate until it thickens to a spreadable consistency.

To make the syrup, combine the water and sugar in small saucepan, bring to the boil and then set asisde.

When your dough is ready, grease or line two 25 × 10 cm (10 × 4 in) loaf tins and divide the dough into two equal pieces. Use a rolling pin to roll out each piece of dough into a rectangle roughly 35 × 30 cm (13¾ × 12 in), with the shortest side parallel to the edge of the bench. Use a spatula to spread half of the chocolate filling over the surface of the dough, leaving a small strip uncovered along the edge furthest from you. This is where you will seal the dough. Sprinkle 50 g (1¾ oz) of chocolate pieces over the filling.

Gently gather the edge closest to you and roll it away from you, like a Swiss roll. Use a pastry brush or wet fingers to brush the uncovered strip at the far edge with water, to seal the roll at the end and stop it from unravelling. Repeat with the other piece of dough and transfer both to a tray lined with baking paper. Cover with a clean, damp tea towel and refrigerate for 15–20 minutes to firm up. This will make it easier to cut.

Take one piece of dough from the fridge and use a sharp knife to cut it in half lengthways. Overlap the strips to make an 'X', with the exposed chocolate filling face up, then twist the pieces over each other like the threads on a screw. You should have at least two twists on either side of the original 'X'. This will create the swirling effect in the baked babka. Place your twist into a tin with the exposed chocolate side up, folding and twisting to fit. Repeat with your second loaf.

Cover the tins with a clean, damp tea towel and leave them in a warm spot to prove for at least 1½ hours. If your kitchen is cool, you can use the oven or an esky as a proofing box by placing a small tray of warm water at the bottom. This creates the humidity and warmth needed. The dough should rise by half. Check that it's proved by gently poking it with one finger. If the indent remains, it's ready; if it springs back quickly, it needs more time.

Towards the end of the prove, preheat the oven to 180°C (360°F). Once ready, place the tins on the top shelf of the oven and bake for 15 minutes before rotating the trays for an even bake. Bake for another 15 minutes, until your babka is golden brown on top. Brush all of the syrup over the top. Leave to cool in the tin for 10 minutes and then transfer to a cooling rack for another 20 minutes before slicing.

Plum bostock

In the tradition of honouring the full potential of any food, bostock was originally created to avoid wasting stale brioche. It is simple to make and highly adaptable. When plums come around we buy them in bulk. We eat them as is for breakfast and after dinner, and use them for simple bakes, where the vivid colour and perfect sweetness shine.

Make the brandy syrup ahead of time so it's cool and ready to go. Always use unwaxed oranges for zesting, so you're not ingesting wax when you eat this.

SEASONS ALTERED

Please don't feel restricted here. Treat this as a guide, or a collection of techniques that you can adapt to your tastes and what's seasonal. Any stone fruit will be sensational on bostock. Berries, figs or poached quince, apple or pear will work perfectly. Select a nut that you like with your chosen fruit.

Serves 8

1 Brioche loaf (page 38)

160 g (5½ oz) Raspberry and lemon thyme jam (page 201)

640 g (1 lb 7 oz) Almond frangipane (page 39)

6–8 plums, halved and sliced

120 g (4½ oz) flaked almonds

icing (confectioners') sugar, for dusting

Brandy syrup

30 g (1 oz) brandy

grated zest and juice of 1 orange

60 g (2 oz) water

50 g (1¾ oz) raw (demerara) sugar

1 cinnamon stick

2 cardamom pods

To make the brandy syrup, combine the brandy, orange zest and juice, water, sugar, cinnamon and cardamom in a small saucepan. Place it over a medium–high heat and bring to the boil, stirring to dissolve the sugar. Set aside to cool and infuse.

Preheat the oven to 180°C (360°F). Line a baking tray with baking paper.

Cut the ends off the brioche loaf and then slice the loaf into 8 slices roughly 2 cm (¾ in) thick. Brush each slice generously with brandy syrup, taking care to get it into the crust. Spread generously with raspberry jam, and then the frangipane. Arrange sliced plum over the surface of each slice and then scatter over the flaked almonds to finish.

Bake your bostock for 25–30 minutes, rotating the tray halfway through to get an even bake. The almonds should be golden, and the edges slightly darker. The frangipane should be firm to touch. Dust with icing sugar before serving.

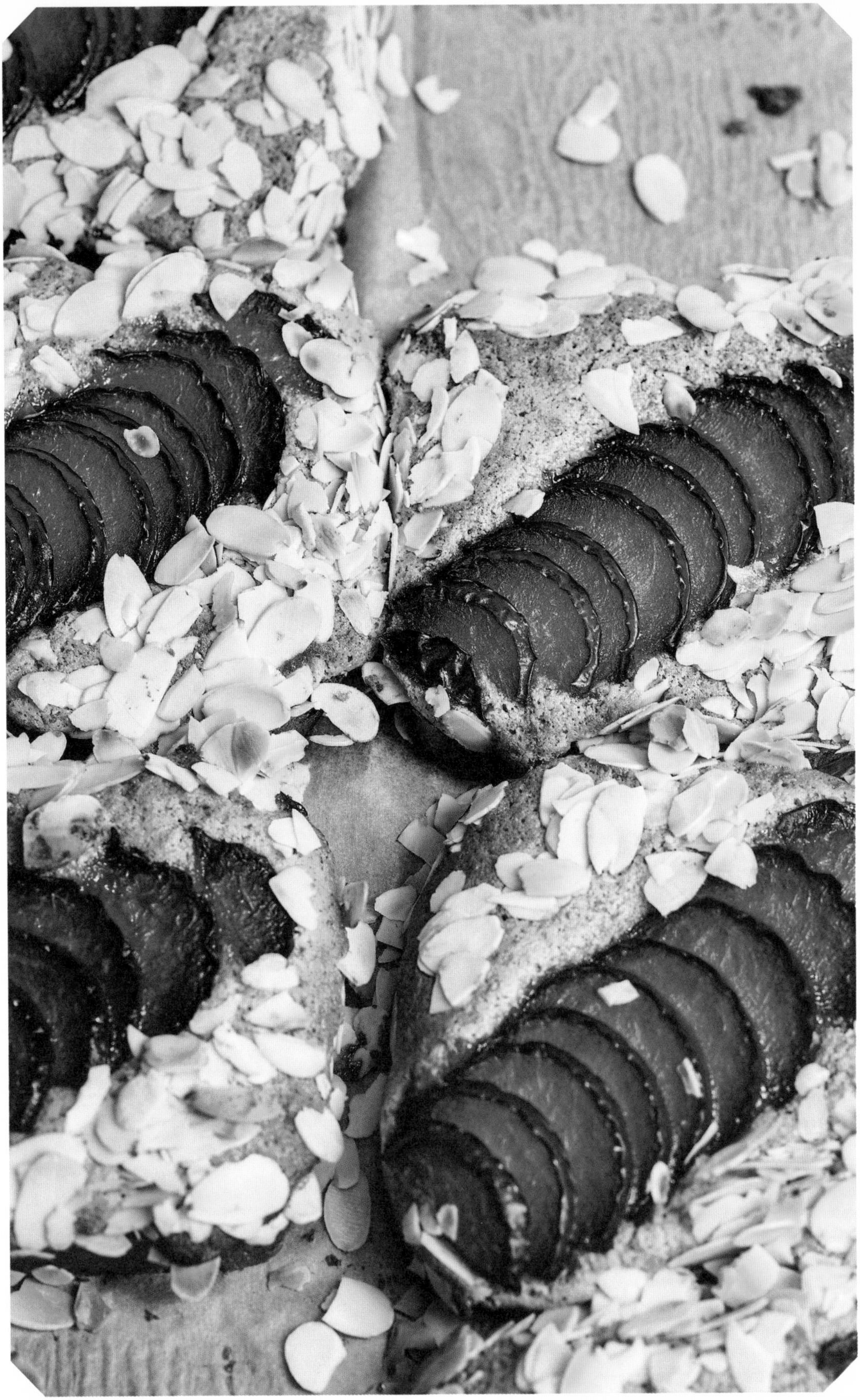

Pistachio and raspberry wagon wheels

Many cultures have a version of a biscuit sandwich. They hold a timeless appeal, being fun to eat and a great way to layer flavour and texture. Chocolate, pistachio and raspberry bounce off each other, and the crisp wholemeal biscuit is a perfect foil for the squishy marshmallow.

Marshmallow was originally made from the root pulp of mallow, found in marshes – hence the name. The marshmallow root has medicinal properties, and was first used by the ancient Egyptians, who boiled the root with honey. This concoction made its way to France, where it was adapted into a squishy confectionery, and from there to America, where it was transformed into the highly processed food we recognise today. This recipe will make more marshmallow than you need for your wagon wheels, because you need the volume of egg whites to get enough air into the mixture. The marshmallow coating is offered so you can make use of the excess – eat it with your hot chocolate or toast it over the campfire.

SEASONS ALTERED

Use your preferred jam and nuts to change up the flavours here.
You can temper your chocolate using the method on page 17 or use a 'cheat's temper'. It's a little quicker and easier, and appropriate for this. Melt 300 g (10½ oz) chocolate over a double boiler. Once melted, take it off the heat and add 15 g (½ oz) of unsalted butter or neutral flavoured oil. Mix until incorporated, and it's ready to use.

Makes 8

1 quantity Wholemeal (whole-wheat) sablé pastry (page 33)

Marshmallow

17 g (⅔ oz) powdered gelatine

205 g (7 oz) water

110 g (4 oz) egg white, at room temperature

200 g (7 oz) caster (superfine) sugar

100 g (3½ oz) honey

¼ teaspoon fine sea salt

1 vanilla bean, seeds scraped (or 1 teaspoon vanilla paste)

Marshmallow coating

30 g (1 oz) cornflour (cornstarch)

100 g (3½ oz) icing (confectioners') sugar

To assemble

160 g (5½ oz) Raspberry and lemon thyme jam (page 201)

300 g (10½ oz) dark chocolate (at least 60% cocoa)

30 g (1 oz) pistachios, roughly chopped

Preheat the oven to 160°C (320°F). Line two baking trays with baking paper.

Roll the pastry out to about 4 mm (¼ in) thick, and use an 8 cm (3¼ in) diameter cutter to cut out 16 circles. Bake for 12 minutes, then rotate the trays and bake for another 2–3 minutes or until the sablé pastry is golden all over. You want the biscuits to be well baked as this will add a bit more texture when you eat the wagon wheel. Set aside to cool on a wire rack.

To make the marshmallow, combine the gelatine and 125 g (4½ oz) of the water at ambient temperature in a small bowl. Set aside. Place the egg whites in the bowl of a stand mixer fitted with the whisk attachment, but don't turn it on yet.

Put the sugar and honey in a small saucepan and add the remaining 80 g (2¾ oz) water. Bring to the boil over a medium–high heat. Many recipes will include high-fructose corn syrup to stop the sugar crystallising, but if you give the pan the occasional shake rather than stirring to dissolve the sugar, it shouldn't crystallise. Use a sugar thermometer to keep an eye on the temperature, and once it reaches 110°C (230°F) start to whisk the egg whites on a medium speed until frothy. Add the salt and keep whisking.

When the sugar gets to 115°C (240°F), turn the mixer up to high speed while keeping a close eye on the sugar. At 118°C (245°F), take it off the heat and gently pour it into the egg whites in a steady stream. Take care to pour in between the bowl and the moving whisk to avoid the hot liquid splashing all over the place.

Once all the sugar syrup has been incorporated, pour the gelatine mixture into the still-warm saucepan to dissolve in the residual heat. Add the vanilla and whisk it in, then pour it in a slow, steady stream into the mixer, once again taking care not to hit the moving whisk and splash it everywhere. Continue to whisk on a high speed for 8–10 minutes or until the bowl is cool to touch. Transfer your marshmallow into a piping bag fitted with a 12 mm (½ in) plain nozzle.

To assemble your wagon wheels, lay your sable discs out on your bench, upside down. Divide the jam between them, placing it in the centre of each disc and then spreading it over the surface, leaving a small gap at the edges. Pipe a layer of marshmallow over half the biscuits, about 2 cm (¾ in) high, again leaving a small gap at the edge. Top with the other half of the biscuits, enclosing the jam and marshmallow, and gently press down so the marshmallow squeezes out a bit, flush with the edge of the biscuit.

Set aside to cool and set the marshmallow.

Make the marshmallow coating by sifting half the cornflour and icing sugar together over a clean tray. Remove the remaining marshmallow from the piping bag and use a spatula to spread it into the tray over the coating. Cover and set aside at room temperature for at least 4 hours, or overnight. Sift the remaining cornflour and icing sugar over the top, then cut the marshmallow into cubes. Toss the cubes in the tray to cover all the cut sides with the coating mixture.

Once the biscuits and marshmallow have set, temper the dark chocolate (page 17). Cover each wagon wheel in chocolate and put it on a wire rack placed over a tray. Sprinkle the pistachio over the top before the chocolate sets. Slide the wagon wheels off the wire rack with a knife, onto a tray lined with baking paper, and store in a cool, dry place for up to 5 days.

Millionaire's shortbread

It's not clear whether the reference to wealth here relates to the caloric value of this chocolate-topped caramel slice, or the fact that sugar and chocolate were out of reach for the average Scottish peasant back in the day. Let's just settle on the fact that this is R I C H. And delicious. A small piece, savoured slowly, is perfect.

Because Millionaire's shortbread is so decadent, it's important to balance the textures and the ratios of biscuit : caramel : chocolate. We've found that a good bite of well-baked shortbread, with a thinner layer of caramel and an even thinner one of chocolate, allows the flavours to shine without leaving you with that slightly sick feeling in your tummy. The wholegrains and oats in the shortbread add character, and a little salt in the caramel is essential.

We find that fresh oats create a superior flavour, and always have oat groats in the panty for rolling. To make oat flour, you can grind rolled oats in a food processor until very fine.

If you're not vigilant in your stirring, you might find that the caramel catches on the bottom of the pan as it reaches the end. Don't panic! And definitely don't throw it away. Just use a sieve to strain the caramel and remove any burnt bits.

SEASONS ALTERED

Save time by using a cheat's temper when you're ready to finish your shortbread (page 17).

Makes 30 bars,
2 × 10 cm (¾ × 4 in)

200 g (7 oz) dark chocolate
  (at least 60% cocoa)
flaky sea salt, for sprinkling

Oat shortbread biscuit

250 g (9 oz) wholemeal
  (whole-wheat) flour
50 g (1¾ oz) oat flour
55 g (2 oz) cornflour (cornstarch)
½ teaspoon fine sea salt
260 g (9 oz) unsalted butter,
  softened
115 g (4 oz) raw (demerara) sugar
1 vanilla bean, seeds scraped
  (or 1 teaspoon vanilla paste)

Salted butter and honey caramel

250 g (9 oz) unsalted butter
65 g (2¼ oz) orange blossom
  honey
60 g (2 oz) raw (demerara) sugar
1 × 340 ml (11½ fl oz) tin
  evaporated milk
½ teaspoon flaky sea salt

To make the shortbread, line a 20 × 30 cm (8 × 12 in) baking tray with baking paper.

Combine the flours and salt in a bowl, then set aside. In a stand mixer fitted with the paddle attachment, beat the butter, sugar and vanilla on a medium speed for 8–10 minutes, until pale and creamy. Add the dry ingredients and mix until just combined. The less you mix, the lighter the base will be.

Transfer the mixture to your baking tray and spread it out evenly, gently pressing down to compact it and ensure it reaches all corners of the tray. You can use a small rolling pin or the bottom of a jar to flatten the surface. Refrigerate for at least 1 hour.

Preheat the oven to 160°C (320°F). Bake your shortbread for 30–35 minutes until the surface is golden all over. Set aside to cool, and turn your attention to the caramel. First, place a small plate in the freezer.

Combine the butter, honey, sugar, evaporated milk and salt in a heavy-based saucepan over a medium heat, stirring frequently as the mixture melts together. Continue to stir as it thickens and darkens, for about 20 minutes until you have large air bubbles spread evenly over the surface. It should be very thick, with the whisk and burst bubbles leaving a mark in the caramel. You can check if it's ready by using the plate test – take your small plate from the freezer, put a small amount of caramel onto the plate and put it in the fridge for 1 minute. Check the consistency by running your finger through the caramel – if it spreads over the plate where your finger was, it needs a bit more time. If your finger leaves a clear mark, it's good to go.

Pour your caramel over the cooled, baked shortbread. Use a spatula to spread it evenly and get it into the corners of the tin, then refrigerate to set.

When the caramel is set, temper your chocolate (page 17). Spread it over the top of the caramel, again using a spatula to achieve an even layer. Sprinkle a little flaky sea salt over the surface just before the chocolate sets, and set aside at room temperature for at least 2 hours.

Transfer your Millionaire's shortbread to a chopping board, and cut into your desired portions.

Baked custard tart

This custard tart is so simple. It relies on the very best ingredients and an eagle eye on the wobble at the end of the bake. There's really nowhere to hide with this bake, so fresh and flavourful dairy and eggs are essential. It takes care to get it right, but when you do it's absolutely sublime. The flavours are so classically English.

Transferring a tart-full of unbaked custard into the oven can result in a mess. If you have an oven with a shelf that slides out, place the tart shell on the shelf, pour the custard in and then carefully slide the shelf back in before closing the door. If not, remove the top shelf of the oven and position the lower one with enough space above it to pour the custard into the tart shell inside the oven. Your kitchen floor will thank you.

SEASONS ALTERED

If you happen upon some duck eggs, by all means use those. Intensely rich, silky and flavoursome, they produce a next-level custard tart.

Serves 12

450 g (1 lb) Sweet pastry (page 25)
730 g (1 lb 10 oz) double
   (heavy) cream
95 g (3¼ oz) full-cream (whole) milk
1 vanilla bean, seeds scraped
   (or 1 teaspoon vanilla paste)
225 g (8 oz) egg yolks
80 g (2¾ oz) caster
   (superfine) sugar
1 whole nutmeg, for grating

Roll the pastry out into a large disc, 3 mm (¼ in) thick. Gently lay it over a 25 cm (10 in) tart case and use your thumb to press it into the corners all the way around. Trim the excess off with a knife, leaving a little overhang to account for shrinkage, then rest it in the fridge for 1 hour.

Preheat the oven to 160°C (320°F). Line the rested pastry case with baking paper and fill with dried beans, rice or coins to weigh the pastry down while you blind bake it. Bake for 25 minutes, then remove the paper and weights and bake for another 5 minutes, until it's a nice light golden colour. Reduce the oven temperature to 110°C (230°F).

Combine the cream, milk and vanilla in a medium saucepan over a low heat. Heat gently, stirring, until warm and combined. In a large mixing bowl, gently whisk the egg yolks and sugar together until combined. Pour the cream mixture slowly over the eggs and sugar, whisking to emulsify. Strain the mixture through a fine sieve into a measuring jug.

Line a tray with baking paper and place the tart shell on top. Place the tray in the oven, then gently pour in the custard and close the door. Bake for 40 minutes until just set. It should have a bit of wobble from the centre, out to a 3–4 cm radius, with the edges more firmly set. Once it starts to set, check it every few minutes to avoid overcooking the custard.

Once cooled, grate the nutmeg over the top before serving.

Seasonal fruit crumble cake

This could be called anything-crumble cake, and it truly expresses the seasons. The base recipe is delicious on its own, lifted by whatever fruit is to hand. Start a day or two ahead, to make the crumble and prepare your fruit, but the actual making of the cake is straightforward. Having a number of elements combined creates layers and interest, but it shouldn't create anxiety. Take the hassle out of your bake by slowing it down and focusing on one thing at a time.

The wholemeal crumble, with the additions of oats and nuts, offers an earthiness and comfort for any season.

Serves 10–12

200 g (7 oz) unsalted butter, softened

170 g (6 oz) caster (superfine) sugar

40 g (1½ oz) muscovado sugar

1 vanilla bean, seeds scraped (or 1 teaspoon vanilla paste)

grated zest of 1 orange or 1 lemon

2 eggs, at room temperature

180 g (6½ oz) plain (all-purpose) flour

60 g (2 oz) wholemeal (whole-wheat) flour

20 g (¾ oz) whole rye flour

1½ teaspoons baking powder

¼ teaspoon fine sea salt

30 g (1 oz) ground almonds

260 g (9 oz) sour cream

ground cinnamon, for sprinkling

your preferred fruit, as below

fresh cream, or extra sour cream, to serve

Crumble topping

125 g (4½ oz) unsalted butter, softened

70 g (2½ oz) ground almonds

55 g (2 oz) raw caster (superfine) sugar

30 g (1 oz) soft brown sugar

70 g (2½ oz) wholemeal (whole-wheat) flour

30 g (1 oz) plain (all-purpose) flour

¼ teaspoon fine sea salt

30 g (1 oz) rolled oats

30 g (1 oz) flaked almonds

To make the crumble topping, combine the butter, ground almonds, sugars, flours and salt in a medium-sized bowl. Use your fingertips to rub the butter into the dry ingredients to create a crumble texture. When it's starting to come together, add the rolled oats and flaked almonds and mix until just incorporated. Transfer to an airtight container and refrigerate until needed.

Preheat the oven to 170°C (340°F). Grease and line a 23 cm (9 in) square or 24 cm (9½ in) round cake tin.

In a stand mixer fitted with the paddle attachment, cream the butter, sugars, vanilla and zest on a medium–high speed for about 10 minutes, until pale and creamy. Lightly whisk the eggs, then add them to the butter mixture in two increments, ensuring each addition is fully incorporated before adding the next. Scrape down the side of the bowl as required to ensure an even mix.

Sift the flours together with the baking powder and salt. When using wholemeal flours you will find bran in the sieve after sifting. The main purpose of sifting is to mix well and knock out any lumps, so just add the bran back in after sifting, along with the ground almonds, and mix well.

Fold the dry mixture into the butter mixture until just combined, then fold in the sour cream and mix until just combined. Transfer to your cake tin and use a spatula to spread the top out evenly. Lightly sprinkle cinnamon over the surface, then add your fruit in one layer and scatter the crumble on top. Spread everything evenly across the surface and all the way to the edges.

Bake on the top shelf of the oven for 50 minutes, then check the cake, rotate the tin and bake for another 10–15 minutes, until a skewer inserted into the middle comes out clean and the crumble is golden all over. Turn out and cool onto a wire rack for 1 hour before serving alongside a jug of fresh cream or with a dollop of sour cream.

SEASONS ALTERED

There are so many ways to adapt this cake. Below are some suggestions.
Spring – 250 g (9 oz) strawberries, hulled and halved
Summer – 4–6 stone fruit, thickly sliced. Nectarine, peach, apricot and plum are all wonderful. Halved fresh figs or 250 g (9 oz) summer berries
Autumn – Apple and blackberry, sliced pear or Poached quinces (page 210). Use 2–3 pome fruit and 100 g (3½ oz) berries
Winter – Wash a bunch of rhubarb and cut into batons. Macerate in raw (demerara) sugar and a little orange juice for 24 hours before assembling your cake.

We've all had a truly ghastly tiramisu. The cloying sweetness, that pasty feeling on the roof of your mouth, the coffee-cream-alcohol balance completely out of whack. It's enough to put a person right off this giant of Italian desserts. But when you taste a truly great tiramisu, it all makes sense. Once again, the genius is in the quality of the simple ingredients, and the right balance of sweetness, bitterness and rich mascarpone cream. A small serve satisfies.

Two of the main ingredients – mascarpone and Savoiardi fingers – are often industrially produced, using ingredients of questionable quality and with added preservatives. If you can make your own, you remove the questions and increase the quality – you will taste and feel the difference. These ingredients are not difficult to make, but they do require some forethought. Start this recipe a few days ahead, and savour each step while removing the stress of getting it all done in one go. It's a lesson in mindful cooking.

This mascarpone recipe is kindly offered by the wonderful cheesemaker Kristen Allan. Kristen shares her considerable cheesy knowledge via intimate classes, one of which Pippa was fortunate to attend. On a journey of home cheese-making, mascarpone is an ideal jumping-off point, requiring only the best pure cream you can find, a simple acid, time and care. Endlessly useful and absolutely delicious.

SEASONS ALTERED

There is some argument about whether tiramisu should contain alcohol, and there are legitimate versions both with and without. As with so many Italian classics, it varies regionally, and everyone's nonna makes the ultimate version. The traditional sweet Marsala adds a layer of sophistication, sitting under the bold main flavours. It's often made with Kahlua or even Tia Maria. We've used stout. Absolutely unconventional and likely the cause of much turning-in-graves, it ups the bitterness and (we think) adds some interest. Any of these choices are absolutely optional.

Serves 8–10

Sponge fingers

3 eggs, separated

75 g (2¾ oz) caster (superfine) sugar

1 vanilla bean, seeds scraped (or 1 teaspoon vanilla paste)

20 g (¾ oz) cornflour (cornstarch)

95 g (3¼ oz) plain (all-purpose) flour

¼ teaspoon fine sea salt

40 g (1½ oz) icing (confectioners') sugar

Preheat the oven to 180°C (360°F). Line two baking trays with baking paper.

To make the sponge fingers, whisk the egg whites in a stand mixer on medium speed until soft peaks form. Add the sugar and continue to whisk for about 5 minutes. Meanwhile, lightly whisk the yolks and vanilla together. In a separate bowl, sift the flours and salt together.

Add the yolks to the whites and continue to mix for another minute. Remove the bowl from the mixer and sift the flour mixture over the egg mixture in 3–4 increments, gently folding in each addition with a spatula before adding the next. Be very gentle, and ensure you reach the bottom and side of the bowl for an even mix.

Transfer the mixture to a piping bag fitted with a 10 mm (½ in) plain nozzle. Pipe 15–16 fingers of mixture onto your lined trays, about 10 cm (4 in) long and 2 cm (¾ in) wide. Dust with icing sugar and set aside for a few minutes for the sugar to settle, creating that crunchy crystallised coating on top. Repeat the dusting of icing sugar just before you put them in the oven. Bake for 10 minutes, then rotate the trays and bake for another 5 minutes, until lightly golden all over. Cool on a wire rack and then set aside until ready to assemble – ideally a couple of days later, when the sponge is slightly stale.

To make the mascarpone, heat the cream over a low–medium heat until it reaches 82°C (180°F). Add the vinegar or lemon juice and stir it in, then continue to stir over the heat until the temperature reaches 90°C (195°F). The cream should eventually thicken into a custard-like consistency and will cover the back of a spoon.

Remove from the heat and cool for 30 minutes at room temperature, then pour into a container and refrigerate overnight.

The next day the mascarpone will look a little thicker but will still be quite runny. Place a colander lined with muslin over a bowl and pour in the cream. Fold the muslin over to cover the cream, then wrap and refrigerate.

After 2 days in the fridge the mascarpone will be lovely and thick, and slightly sour. Transfer it to an airtight container and store in the fridge. Use within 14 days.

Mascarpone

500 g (1 lb 2 oz) double
(heavy) cream

20 g (¾ oz) apple-cider vinegar
or lemon juice

Mascarpone cream

5 eggs, separated

160 g (5½ oz) caster
(superfine) sugar

1 vanilla bean, seeds scraped
(or 1 teaspoon vanilla paste)

400 g (14 oz) mascarpone
(see above)

To assemble

200 g (7 oz) espresso

50 g (1¾ oz) stout or sweet
Marsala (optional)

cocoa powder, for dusting

40 g (1½ oz) dark chocolate
(at least 60% cocoa), for shaving

40 g (1½ oz) cacao nibs

To make the mascarpone cream, put the egg yolks, sugar and vanilla in a stand mixer fitted with the whisk attachment, and whisk on medium–high speed for 10 minutes, until pale, thick and glossy. Add the mascarpone and whisk until soft peaks form. Transfer to another bowl and refrigerate while you clean the mixer bowl and whisk the egg whites on medium speed for about 3 minutes until soft peaks form.

Gently fold the egg whites into the mascarpone mixture in two additions. Transfer to an airtight container and refrigerate until you're ready to assemble the tiramisu.

Use a 22 cm (8¾ in) square or 24 cm (9½ in) round dish to assemble your tiramisu. Combine the espresso with the alcohol, if using. Dip the sponge fingers in the liquid for a few seconds on each side, to lightly soak them. You don't want them drowning in coffee, just a touch. Lay half of your soaked sponge fingers over the base of your dish, and cover with half of the mascarpone cream. Add another layer of soaked sponge, and then the remaining cream. Finish with a dusting of cocoa powder, shavings of dark chocolate and cacao nibs for a little crunch.

Seasons
shared

Stories told through food

Pages 131–63

The recipes that we return to tell the stories that shape our lives. Meals shared with loved ones, recipes traded for fruit between neighbours to share the spoils of a seasonal glut, potluck picnics with friends new and old. Food can tell stories of family left behind in far-off lands, of deep cultural connections, or of a childhood spent gathering the fruits of the season in a landscape inseparable from the people who know and love it. Ask someone why they cook a certain dish and you'll glimpse their soul in the answer.

Many of these recipes are quite literally designed to share – simple tarts and cakes can be the star of the picnic or the smash hit at the school bake sale. Sweet pies loaded with fruit look spectacular and are deeply comforting, creating visceral memories in the eating. The beautiful peach and rosemary galette conveys the essence of the way we cook. With a little technique and the very best ingredients, it's perfect for any occasion. These bakes are easily transportable, and expressive of their place and time. Share them widely.

We're grateful for the enormous culinary diversity of where we live, as well as the opportunities we've had to travel and experience many cultures. Access to culturally appropriate foods creates safety within communities, and empathy when shared more broadly. In these turbulent times, we could do worse than sharing our food cultures and the stories that go with them. Here, we're delighted to share recipes from friends of diverse cultures – Rugelach, Linzer torte tartlets, sour cherry Florentines, Basque cheesecake and the incredible spiced brown ale pudding, which all come from bakers and chefs we greatly admire. These recipes have been generously shared with us, and we're including them here so they can continue to weave their magic far and wide.

Breaking bread with others is an intimate invitation to share. Individually plated desserts like a brown ale pudding with salted caramel sauce or a classic rum baba are ideal for entertaining – both can be prepared in advance, are simple to make and fancy enough to impress your friends. Another baked pudding, the blood plum clafoutis, is a straightforward bake but no less impressive and expressive of the season.

There is much to be gained by pausing to savour the stories woven into the food we eat. We form a connection to the land by choosing to eat produce in the season that it ripens. Connection to people comes through experiencing their culture and listening to their stories. Barriers are broken and lifelong bonds are formed. The power of sharing food and stories is immense.

Cream cheese Rugelach

Rugelach are sweet, filled pastries originating in the Jewish communities of Poland. They're shaped like a small croissant, but the similarity ends there – this is a fairly simple bake, and far less time consuming. The flaky sour cream pastry is rolled with apricot jam, currants and chocolate to create little sweet treats with joy in every bite. Michael grew to love these while working with Maaryasha Werdiger at her incredible bakery, Zelda. Maaryasha makes beautiful breads and pastries that connect her grateful community to their cultural origins.

For best results, make the pastry by hand. As with many things, less is more here: minimal mixing will create a flaky and delicate pastry. Mixing by hand means you get to feel the dough, only just bringing it together. If you're working ahead, you can freeze the rolled pastry pieces in an airtight container. Bake from frozen, adding a few minutes to the bake time.

Rugelach is a wonderful morning indulgence, freshly baked and served with strong coffee.

SEASONS ALTERED

With the Jewish diaspora spread far and wide, you can find many variations in the pastry and fillings for Rugelach. Raisin and walnut is popular, as are poppy seeds or different fruit preserves.

Makes 12

20 g (¾ oz) soft brown sugar

½ teaspoon ground cinnamon

30 g (1 oz) chocolate chips

40 g (1½ oz) walnuts, lightly toasted and roughly chopped

30 g (1 oz) currants

1 teaspoon lemon juice

60 g (2 oz) Apricot and amaretto jam (page 204)

raw (demerara) sugar, for sprinkling

Cream cheese pastry

140 g (5 oz) plain (all-purpose) flour

2 g (¹⁄₁₆ oz) fine sea salt

grated zest of 1 small lemon

100 g (3½ oz) unsalted butter, chilled, cut into 3 cm (1¼ in) dice

100 g (3½ oz) full-fat cream cheese, chilled

Egg wash

1 egg

splash of full-cream (whole) milk

pinch of fine sea salt

To make the pastry, combine the flour, salt, lemon zest and butter in a medium-sized bowl and toss it all together. Tip the mixture onto your bench. Using a rolling pin, roll the butter into the flour until you have a shaggy crumble with large shards of butter still visible. Break up the cream cheese and add it to your pile. Slide a dough scraper underneath one side of the mixture and fold it over itself, then repeat from the other side, bringing it together with your other hand and continuing to mix until it all just comes together. There should still be streaks of butter and cream cheese visible. Wrap the dough and refrigerate for at least 1 hour, or preferably overnight.

To prepare the filling, combine the soft brown sugar, cinnamon, chocolate chips, walnuts, currants and lemon juice in a medium-sized bowl and mix well.

When you are ready to assemble the Rugelach, remove the pastry from the fridge and roll it out into a disc about 30 cm (12 in) in diameter and 3 mm (⅛ in) thick. Spread the apricot jam evenly over the surface and then generously sprinkle the filling over the top. Use a sharp knife to cut it like a pizza, creating 12 wedges of roughly equal size.

Line two baking trays with baking paper. Take one slice and roll from the outer edge towards the point, creating a mini croissant shape. Place it on a tray, seam side down, and then repeat with the remaining slices, leaving a gap of 4 cm (1½ in) between each one. Refrigerate for 1 hour.

Preheat the oven to 180°C (360°F). Make the egg wash by lightly whisking the egg, milk and salt together. When the oven is hot, remove the trays from the fridge and brush each pastry with egg wash. Sprinkle with demerara sugar and bake for 12 minutes, then turn the tray and bake for another 4–6 minutes, until golden and flaky Don't worry if the filling oozes out a bit – this will caramelise a little, giving a lovely toffee taste. Cool slightly and serve warm.

Store in an open container, loosely covered with foil so the sugar doesn't weep, for up to 4 days.

Cream buns

These cream buns are simple and old-fashioned, often overlooked or under-appreciated in favour of fancier (or trendier) bakes. The super-light dough filled with soft whipped cream and a smear of jam is like a little cloud of fruity sweetness. Heaven. Cream buns make a perfect afternoon tea treat. They also travel well, making them ideal for picnics and potluck gatherings.

SEASONS ALTERED

To create an extra light and fluffy brioche, use the tangzhong method. Boil 40 g (1½ oz) of the milk and pour it over 40 g (1½ oz) of the flour, barely mixing. Set aside to cool before mixing your dough, adding it in with the remaining flour and milk. The liquid will absorb the starch, causing it to swell and gelatinise, resulting in a light, spongy crumb when baked. This method can also be used for doughs such as milk bread, brioche or hot cross buns.

Makes 16

240 g (8½ oz) full-cream (whole) milk

400 g (14 oz) bakers (strong) flour

60 g (2 oz) honey

8 g (¼ oz) instant dried yeast

1 medium egg, at room temperature

6 g (⅕ oz) fine sea salt

80 g (2¾ oz) unsalted butter, roughly chopped and softened

400 g (14 oz) double (heavy) cream

1 vanilla bean, seeds scraped (or 1 teaspoon vanilla paste)

10 g (¼ oz) icing (confectioners') sugar

400 g (14 oz) Strawberry and lemon verbena jam (page 200)

Egg wash

1 egg

splash of full-cream (whole) milk

pinch of fine sea salt

Combine the milk with the flour, honey, yeast, egg and salt in the mixing bowl of a stand mixer fitted with the dough hook. Mix on a low speed for 5 minutes to incorporate the ingredients, stopping occasionally to scrape down the side of the bowl.

Check the consistency; it should be like slightly sticky playdough. Increase the speed to medium and mix for a further 5 minutes, then add the butter all at once. Don't worry about overcrowding the bowl – it will all work itself out and mix through.

Continue to mix on a medium speed for another 8 minutes. You may need to stop to scrape down the side of the bowl a few times. Mix until your dough comes away from the side of the bowl and is velvety and smooth. You should be able to stretch it out without it breaking.

Cover and set aside for 1 hour, ideally at around 22–24°C (72–75°F). If your kitchen is too cold, put it in your (cold) oven with a light on, with a pan of hot water at the bottom to create warmth and humidity.

After 1 hour, give the dough a fold.

To do this, wet or oil your hands and grab a piece of dough on the side of the bowl. Pull and stretch it up over the middle to the other side of the bowl. Repeat this 6–8 times, moving around the edge of the bowl. You can also knead the dough on the benchtop.

Cover once more and set aside at room temperature to prove for another hour or so, until it has risen. When you shake the bowl the dough should wobble a little, and feel light and full of air. Check if it's ready by gently poking the dough. If your fingertip leaves a dent, it's ready, but if the dough springs back quickly, cover it again and give it more time.

Once the dough is ready, shape, prove and bake your buns. Line two baking trays with baking paper. Tip the dough onto a lightly floured bench and divide it into 16 equal pieces, about 50 g (1¾ oz) each. Knock out any large bubbles in each piece and then shape them into balls. To do this, place your dominant hand over a piece of dough and apply downwards pressure as you move your hand in a circular motion, rotating the dough in your palm. Applying pressure as you shape the bun builds strength in the dough and makes it more taut. This should take about 30 seconds. Repeat with the remaining dough pieces, placing them on the lined trays about 6 cm (2½ in) apart.

Loosely cover the trays with plastic wrap and prove at 22–24°C (72–75°F) for 1 hour, or until risen by half. About 40 minutes into the final prove, preheat the oven to 170°C (340°F). Pour about 150 g (5½ oz) water into a tray at the bottom of the oven.

Check the buns – they should wobble slightly when you shake the tray. Test them by gently pressing the surface. If your fingertip leaves a dent, they're ready to bake, but if the dough springs back quickly, they need more time.

Make the egg wash by lightly whisking the egg, milk and salt together. Lightly brush each bun with egg wash. Bake for 7 minutes, and then swap the trays and rotate them. Remove the tray of water and bake for another 5–7 minutes. The buns should be a deep golden colour. Transfer to a wire rack to cool.

When you are ready to assemble your buns, whip the cream with the vanilla and icing sugar until soft peaks form. Cut each bun in half diagonally, leaving the top and bottom attached to form a hinge. Generously spread the base of each with jam and then spoon a big dollop of cream on top and close the lid. Gently press the top down so the jam and cream spread to the edges, and then dust the top with icing sugar. These are best eaten on the day they're made.

Lemon tart

There's a particular challenge in perfecting a very simple bake that is part of its timeless appeal. Lemon tart is all about the moment when you achieve that gentle wobble in the middle and then remove it from the oven, allowing the residual heat to finish it off. The resulting silky smooth, tart-sweet filling is something to behold.

Precision in the proportions will help here, which is why we always weigh the eggs for this recipe. Overly large eggs can also create an eggy flavour in the baked tart. The tart shell can be blind baked ahead of time, and stored in an airtight container at room temperature for up to 1 week.

SEASONS ALTERED

Meyer lemons will produce a very different result here. Less tart and slightly more rounded in flavour, Meyers are ideal for sweet bakes when in season. The zest of a Meyer lemon is less delicious than that of other lemons, so combine the mellow juice of the Meyer with the zest of something like a Eureka lemon for zing.

Serves 12

½ quantity of Sweet pastry (page 25)
350 g (12½ oz) caster (superfine) sugar
grated zest of 4 lemons
450 g (1 lb) eggs, at room temperature
250 g (9 oz) lemon juice
250 g (9 oz) double (heavy) cream

Egg wash

1 egg
splash of full-cream (whole) milk
pinch of fine sea salt

Grease a 25 cm (10 in) tart tin. Roll your rested pastry out into a large disc 3 mm (⅛ in) thick, and gently lay it over the tin. Use your thumbs to press the pastry into the corners of the tin, leaving the edges overhanging a little to allow for some shrinkage. Keep any unused pastry for another use, wrapped and refrigerated. Refrigerate the lined tart case for 20 minutes and preheat the oven to 190°C (375°F).

When the oven is hot, line the tart case with foil and fill with baking weights – granulated sugar is ideal for this because it gets right into the corners. Bake for 25 minutes, and then remove the foil and baking weights. Reduce the heat to 160°C (320°F) and bake for another 10 minutes, until the pastry is golden all over. Check for any gaps or cracks, and plug those with excess raw pastry. Make the egg wash by lightly whisking the egg, milk and salt together. Lightly brush the entire surface of the shell with egg wash and return it to the oven for a few more minutes. The egg wash will help create a seal to avoid leakages later on. When cool enough to handle, use a vegetable peeler or sharp serrated knife to trim the pastry neatly down to the edge of the tart tin. Set aside until needed.

Preheat the oven to 130°C (265°F).

Combine the sugar and lemon zest in a bowl and rub them together to mix well and distribute the oils. In a separate bowl, lightly whisk the eggs before adding the sugar, then whisk to combine. Strain the lemon juice and add to the egg mixture, whisking to combine. Leave to sit for 5 minutes to dissolve the sugar. Finally, add the cream and whisk to combine. Strain the mixture into a jug.

Place your empty tart shell on a tray on the middle shelf of the oven. Give the filling a little whisk and then slowly pour it into the shell, right to the top. Skim or pop any big bubbles that appear. Gently close the oven door and bake for 45 minutes, then check the tart by gently wobbling the tray. If it still seems very liquid in the middle, cook for another 5–10 minutes, checking it every minute or two. To achieve the sweet spot, timing is crucial – you are looking for a slight wobble, kind of like jelly, from the centre of the tart, out to a 3–4 cm radius, with the edges more firmly set. Remove it from the oven and set it aside; the residual heat will finish the cooking.

Lemon tart is best served on the day it is baked, slightly warm from the oven. It's delicious served with a spoonful of Berry and rose geranium compote (page 198) or fresh berries and a dollop of crème fraîche.

Chocolate tart

This is a lovely recipe to show off your skills and highlight great-quality chocolate. Michael first made it at Pied à Terre in London, a two-Michelin-starred restaurant then headed by chef Tom Aikens. From there it's travelled with him, to bakeries and restaurants, to our home and now to you.

Ethical chocolate is having a moment, and there are more and more micro producers popping up, fascinated by the process of roasting and conching the bean into bars that express their origin and personality. If you can find locally produced chocolate of a high quality, use that. Ask questions about their sourcing; chocolate is an industry rife with exploitation and greenwashing, at the mercy of the stock exchange. By buying carefully sourced chocolate from a small local business, you can support a close supply chain and contribute to a positive livelihood for people in your community and at the source.

SEASONS ALTERED

We sometimes use cacao nibs to garnish this tart as well as or instead of grated dark chocolate. They give a lovely crunch and bitterness that works well with the richness of the tart filling.

Serves 12

½ quantity Sweet pastry (page 25)
240 g (8½ oz) full-cream (whole) milk
400 g (14 oz) double (heavy) cream
500 g (1 lb 2 oz) good-quality dark chocolate (at least 70%)
3 (150 g/5½ oz) whole eggs

Egg wash

1 egg
splash of full-cream (whole) milk
pinch of flaky sea salt

To finish

20–40 g (¾–1½ oz) dark chocolate (at least 60% cocoa), for grating
flaky sea salt, for sprinkling

Grease a 25 cm (10 in) tart tin. Roll your rested pastry out into a large disc 3 mm (⅛ in) thick, and gently lay it over the tin. Use your thumbs to press the pastry into the corners of the tin, leaving the edges overhanging a little to allow for some shrinkage. Keep any excess pastry for another use, wrapped and refrigerated. Refrigerate the lined tart case for 20 minutes and preheat the oven to 190°C (375°F).

When the oven is hot, line the tart case with foil and fill with baking weights – granulated sugar is ideal for this because it gets right into the corners. Bake for 25 minutes and then remove the foil and baking weights. Reduce the heat to 160°C (320°F) and bake for another 10 minutes, until the pastry is golden all over. Check for any gaps or cracks, and plug those with excess raw pastry. Make the egg wash by lightly whisking the egg, milk and salt together.

Lightly brush the entire surface of the shell with egg wash and return it to the oven for a few more minutes. The egg wash will help create a seal to avoid leakage later on. When cool enough to handle, use a vegetable peeler or sharp serrated knife to trim the pastry neatly down to the edge of the tart tin. Set aside until needed.

Preheat the oven to 110°C (230°F).

Combine the milk and cream in a saucepan over a low–medium heat. Bring it just to a simmer, then remove from the heat and set aside to cool.

Put the chocolate in a medium sized bowl over a saucepan of simmering water, ensuring the water doesn't touch the bowl. Keeping the heat low, melt the chocolate, being careful not to overheat it. Once melted, remove from the heat and set aside to cool slightly.

Lightly beat the eggs in a small bowl, and then add to the melted chocolate. Whisk to combine and then add the cooled milk and cream. Use a spatula to bring it all together and then transfer the mixture into a jug.

Place your empty tart shell on a tray on the middle shelf of the oven. Slowly pour the mixture into the shell, right to the top. Gently close the oven door and bake for 30 minutes. Check the tart and carefully turn the tin to get an even bake, then bake for another 15–20 minutes, until just set. Keep a close eye on it towards the end of the bake. You are looking for a slight wobble in the centre of the tart – the residual heat will finish it off out of the oven. Cool for an hour on a wire rack.

Coarsely grate dark chocolate over the surface of the tart and sprinkle with flaky sea salt. Serve with a good spoonful of crème fraîche or sour cream. Store in an airtight container in the fridge for up to 4 days.

Bakewell tart

The Bakewell is a British classic, hailing from the northern county of Derbyshire. Originally a pudding, it has evolved into tart form and commonly consists of a sweet tart shell filled with layers of jam, almond cream and fruit, making it very adaptable to the seasons. It's a beautifully easy and flexible bake, wonderful for sharing.

Always leave space for the frangipane to rise during baking as it can overspill, especially if it has been well aerated through mixing.

SEASONS ALTERED

When the first flush of strawberries comes through in spring, use 500 g (1 lb 2 oz) strawberries over blackberry jam. In summer, use a foundation of raspberry jam, and top with 6–8 fresh apricots or plums. Top the same base with 6–8 figs or slices of poached quince or pear in autumn. For your winter Bakewell, lay the base with strawberry jam and finish with fresh rhubarb macerated in a little sugar.

Serves 12

½ quantity Sweet pastry (page 25)

100 g (3½ oz) jam of your choice

700 g (1 lb 9 oz) Almond frangipane, softened (page 39)

seasonal fresh fruit

100 g (3½ oz) flaked almonds

Grease a 25 cm (10 in) tart tin. Roll your rested pastry out into a large disc 3 mm (⅛ in) thick, and gently lay it over the tin. Use your thumbs to press the pastry into the corners of the tin, leaving the edges overhanging a little to allow for some shrinkage. Keep any excess pastry for another use, wrapped and refrigerated. Refrigerate the lined tart case for 20 minutes and preheat the oven to 190°C (375°F).

When the oven is hot, line the tart case with foil and fill with baking weights – granulated sugar is ideal for this because it gets right into the corners. Bake for 20 minutes and then remove the foil and baking weights. Reduce the heat to 160°C (320°F) and bake for another 6–8 minutes, until the pastry is cooked but still pale. Check for any gaps or cracks, and plug those with excess raw pastry. When cool enough to handle, use a vegetable peeler or sharp serrated knife to trim the pastry neatly down to the edge of the tart tin. Set aside to cool.

Preheat the oven to 160°C (320°F). Spoon the jam into the tart shell and spread it across the base, then spread the frangipane evenly over the jam. It should reach about 5 mm (¼ in) from the top, allowing space for it to rise during baking. Arrange the fruit over the surface, pressing it down very gently, and then scatter the flaked almonds over the top. Bake on the top shelf of the oven for 30 minutes and then rotate it to ensure an even bake. Bake for another 5–10 minutes, until firm to touch. If, at the point when you turn the tin, the pastry is getting too dark but the frangipane is not baked, reduce the heat to 150°C (300°F) for the remainder of the bake.

Cool on a wire rack for 30 minutes before serving. Store in an airtight container at room temperature for up to 5 days.

Thomas and Gabi Moritz operate Boonderoo Farm, an organic farm and bakery in Victoria's High Country. There, they produce bakes made with fresh flour, milled on site, and much of their menu is home grown. They believe fervently in whole food, highly nutritious and full of flavour, and who can argue when it tastes as good as this? These spelt and hazelnut Linzer torte tartlets hold the story of their origin in Austria, and also that of the place where they landed, on the other side of the world.

SEASONS ALTERED

There are many fillings you could add to make this your own. Raspberry, spelt and hazelnut is wonderful; redcurrant, plum or a cherry preserve are also great. A rye pastry will give a deeper flavour that's fantastic with red fruits – just replace 25 per cent of the spelt flour with rye.

Makes 8

400 g (14 oz) jam of your choice

Spiced spelt and hazelnut pastry

250 g (9 oz) unsalted butter, softened
250 g (9 oz) whole spelt flour
250 g (9 oz) hazelnut meal
150 g (5½ oz) caster (superfine) sugar
1 teaspoon ground cinnamon
1 teaspoon cloves
1 teaspoon lemon zest
1 medium egg, at room temperature
1 egg yolk, at room temperature
approximately 70 g (2½ oz) full-cream (whole) milk

In the bowl of a stand mixer fitted with the paddle attachment, combine the butter, spelt flour, hazelnut meal, sugar, spices and lemon zest. Mix on medium speed until it just comes together. Add the whole egg and yolk, and mix until combined. Tip the dough onto your bench and gently knead to bring the dough all together. If you find the dough is still a bit dry, add another egg yolk and mix until just combined. Flatten the dough into a disc, wrap it and then rest in the fridge for 20 minutes.

While the pastry is resting, preheat the oven to 160°C (320°F) and lightly grease 8 tart moulds, 10 cm (4 in) in diameter. Weigh out eight pieces of pastry, 60 g (2 oz) each. Roll each piece into a disc slightly bigger than the mould and use your fingers to press it into the corners so that it covers the mould evenly all over.

Weigh the remaining dough, calculate 15 per cent of that weight, and then add that weight in milk. For example, if you have 470 g (1 lb 1 oz) dough left after weighing out your ten pieces, add 70 g (2½ oz) of milk. Beat the remaining dough and milk together in your stand mixer, fitted with the paddle attachment, until well combined. Transfer this looser dough mixture into a piping bag fitted with a small nozzle.

Fill each tart with jam, spreading it evenly to just under the rim. Pipe the remaining pastry into a lattice pattern over the top of each tart. Any leftover dough or trimmings can be frozen for later use.

Bake for 35 minutes, then rotate the tray and reduce the temperature to 150°C (300°F). Bake for another 10 minutes, until deep golden all over. Once baked, leave to cool for 10 minutes before serving. Your tarts will keep in an airtight container for up to 4 days.

A Florentine is a fruit and nut lover's treat, dipped in chocolate. This recipe was kindly shared with us by Justine Kajtar of Red Door Corner Store, so that we could share it with you. A wonderful combination of nuts with bursts of tart sour cherries, held in a decadent chewy caramel, these are amazing in the morning with coffee, and totally addictive. Please enjoy responsibly.

The caramel will spread like crazy during baking if allowed, so you will need eight stainless steel rings, 8 cm (3¼ in) in diameter, to hold the mixture in a perfect circle. You will also need a sugar thermometer.

SEASONS ALTERED

Glacé ginger is magnificent with chocolate and almonds, and makes a delicious alternative, although it can't really be called a Florentine. A combination of other nuts will also work well in this recipe. It's all interchangeable, so make it your own. Just keep the quantities similar to achieve the desired consistency.

And while we like lining ours with dark chocolate, try using milk or even white chocolate for something a little different.

Makes 8

80 g (2¾ oz) unsalted butter

80 g (2¾ oz) caster
   (superfine) sugar

5 g (1/8 oz) flaky sea salt

60 g (2 oz) honey

90 g (3 oz) double (heavy) cream

200 g (7 oz) flaked almonds

60 g (2 oz) dried sour cherries,
   roughly chopped

50 g (1¾ oz) pistachios,
   roughly chopped

150 g (5½ oz) dark chocolate

Preheat the oven to 160°C (320°F) and line a baking tray with baking paper. Lightly grease eight 8 cm (3¼ in) stainless steel rings with butter or oil and place them on the tray.

Combine the butter, sugar, salt, honey and cream in a saucepan over a medium heat. Slowly caramelise the mixture, stirring frequently with a wooden spoon as it heats up. Continue to heat, stirring constantly once the temperature is over 100°C (210°F) to prevent the cream from burning.

When the temperature reaches 120°C (250°F), remove the pan from the heat and add the almonds, sour cherries and pistachios. Mix well, then immediately divide the mixture evenly between your steel rings. Bake for 14–15 minutes until the surface is golden caramel in colour. Leave to cool completely on the tray.

When you are ready to finish your Florentines, line a baking tray with baking paper. Place your Florentines on the tray, smooth side up. Melt the chocolate in a bowl set over a saucepan with a little water in the bottom, over a low heat. Be careful not to let the chocolate get too hot. Stir occasionally as it melts, and remove from the heat when done.

Spoon a little melted chocolate onto each Florentine and spread it evenly over the top, right to the edge. Just before the chocolate sets, swirl a pastry scraper comb (or the prongs of a fork) through each Florentine, then leave to set in a cool dry place. Store in an airtight container for up to 5 days. They will soften a little over time in humid conditions.

Strawberry, rhubarb and pistachio tart

There's something bewitching about the combination of red fruits and rosewater. The fragrance is incredible, and the spiced pistachio pastry adds to the allure. We've been baking this for years, always in spring when strawberries first reappear at the market. We buy beautiful rhubarb from Ramarro Farm, bright red and flavoursome. We've tweaked the pastry over the years, and will also tweak the filling at different times of the year. We invite friends over to give us an excuse to make this tart, and it never fails to impress.

SEASONS ALTERED

The first strawberries that come through in spring are a delight, ambrosial and sweet. When they're this good, double the strawberries and leave the rhubarb out. At the height of summer, yellow peaches are a wonderful fruit for the filling; perhaps switch out the pistachios for almonds in the pastry.

Serves 8–10

350 g (12½ oz) strawberries, hulled and halved

400 g (14 oz) rhubarb, sliced into 1 cm (½ in) pieces on an angle

100 g (3½ oz) raw (demerara) sugar

30 g (1 oz) cornflour (cornstarch)

grated zest of 1 orange

20 g (¾ oz) orange juice

20 g (¾ oz) rosewater

icing (confectioners') sugar, for dusting

Pastry

225 g (8 oz) unsalted butter, chilled

270 g (9½ oz) plain (all-purpose) flour

80 g (2¾ oz) ground pistachios

80 g (2¾ oz) caster (superfine) sugar

5 g (⅛ oz) fine sea salt

2 teaspoons ground cinnamon

½ teaspoon ground star anise

grated zest of 1 orange

3 egg yolks, at room temperature

Egg wash

1 egg

splash of full-cream (whole) milk

pinch of fine sea salt

To make the pastry, cut the butter into 1 cm (½ in) dice and chill it in the freezer while you weigh out the rest of your ingredients.

Put the flour, ground pistachios, sugar, salt, spices and orange zest in a bowl and whisk with a fork to combine and knock out any lumps. Turn out the mixture onto a clean bench and scatter the chilled butter cubes over the top. Using a rolling pin, roll the butter into the flour, gathering the flour back into the middle with a dough scraper as you go. Keep rolling until the mixture has a crumbly texture, with pea-sized lumps or shards of butter still visible.

Lightly whisk the yolks, then make a well in the middle of the dry ingredients and add the yolks. Use a dough scraper or spoon to gently cut the flour into the yolks until you have an even crumble texture, gathering up any leaks as you do. Use your fingertips to gently push it all together into a rough dough with a slightly sticky texture. If it feels dry, add fridge-cold milk or water 1 tablespoon at a time until there are no floury bits left.

Roll or press the pastry out into a rectangle roughly 2–3 cm (¾–1¼ in) thick (exact dimensions are not important here). Fold one-third of the pastry into the middle, then the other third over the top of that, as if folding a letter. Rotate the pastry 90 degrees and roll it out again, into a rectangle roughly 2–3 cm (¾–1¼ in) thick and repeat the letter fold. Don't worry about making these folds perfectly neat – this is just to finish bringing the dough together and layer the butter, which results in a lovely flakiness. If it's still a bit dry or floury, add a bit of water as you go.

Rotate and roll the pastry out once more into a rectangle 2–3 cm (¾–1¼ in) thick and do one last fold. Wrap and refrigerate for at least 1 hour or overnight.

Grease a 36 × 13 cm (14¼ × 5 in) rectangular tart tin. Roll two-thirds of the pastry into a rectangle 3–4 mm (⅛–¼ in) thick and large enough to fill your tart tin. Gently lay the pastry over the tin and press it into the corners. Trim the edges, leaving a little overhang for shrinkage. Roll the remaining third of the pastry between two sheets of baking paper, into a rectangle 3–4 mm (⅛ in) thick with the short edge around 15 cm (6 in) long. Put it and your lined tart tin in the fridge to rest for at least 1 hour.

Preheat the oven to 160°C (320°F). Combine the strawberries, rhubarb, sugar, cornflour, zest and juice and rosewater in a bowl, and mix well.

Make the egg wash by lightly whisking the egg, milk and salt together. Remove the rectangle of pastry from the fridge and cut it into strips 2 cm (¾ in) wide, widthways – you can use a pastry wheel cutter for a serrated edge, if you have one. Remove the tart case from the fridge and transfer the fruit mixture into it, spreading it out evenly. Arrange the strips of pastry over the fruit into diagonal crosses. Once you've laid all your strips, gently press the ends into the base and brush the top with egg wash. Bake for 50–60 minutes, until the pastry is crisp and golden. Cool in the tin for half an hour, then remove and cool to room temperature. Dust the top with icing sugar and serve with fresh mascarpone (page 127).

Peach and rosemary galette

A galette is simple to make and joyous to eat. Peach and rosemary are fantastic together, and the spelt in the pastry provides a slightly nutty element that is perfectly complementary.

Whether you're a novice or a professional pastry chef, galettes are a super satisfying bake. We always have some galette pastry in the freezer. It's so versatile and delicious.

SEASONS ALTERED

The galette pastry provides a foundation for almost endless possibilities, allowing you to capture the best of any season in this beautiful, rustic free-form tart.

Below are some ideas for galettes through the seasons.
Spring – strawberry and fennel pollen, cherry and almond
Summer – apricots, figs and any stone fruit work best
Autumn – apple galettes are a classic
Winter – rhubarb and orange
You can make individual galettes by dividing the dough and filling by six and following the instructions below, in miniature.

Serves 6

6 medium-sized ripe peaches
2 sprigs rosemary
90 g (3 oz) raw (demerara) sugar
½ vanilla bean, seeds scraped,
    or ½ teaspoon vanilla bean paste
½ teaspoon ground cinnamon
raw sugar, for sprinkling

Pastry

225 g (8 oz) unsalted butter, cut into
    1 cm (½ in) dice
250 g (9 oz) wholegrain spelt flour
100 g (3½ oz) plain
    (all-purpose) flour
¾ teaspoon fine sea salt
120 g (4½ oz) crème fraîche
    or sour cream
2 teaspoons water, chilled

Egg wash

1 egg
splash of full-cream (whole) milk
pinch of fine sea salt

Chill the butter in the freezer while you prepare the rest of your ingredients. Sift together the flours and salt onto a clean bench, then scatter the cubed butter over the top. Using a rolling pin, roll the butter into the flour, gathering the flour in as you go. Keep rolling until the mixture has a crumbly texture, with pea-sized lumps of butter still visible. Transfer the mixture to a large mixing bowl and make a well in the middle.

In a separate bowl, lightly whisk the crème fraîche or sour cream and water together, then pour them into the well. Use a spoon to gently 'cut' the flour into the wet mix until you have an even crumble texture. Using your fingertips, gently push it together into a rough dough. It should have a thick, smooth and slightly sticky texture. Place the dough on a lightly floured bench and roll it out into a rectangle roughly 2 cm (¾ in) thick, with the long edge towards you.

Fold one-third of the pastry into the middle, then the other third over the top of that, as if folding a letter. Rotate the pastry 90 degrees and roll it out again, into a rectangle roughly 2 cm (¾ in) thick. Repeat the letter fold. Roll the pastry out once more into a rectangle 2 cm (¾ in) thick, then wrap it in plastic wrap and rest it in the fridge for 1 hour.

Remove the pastry from the fridge and roll it out between two sheets of baking paper, into a rounded shape 4 mm (⅛ in) thick. Return it to the fridge for another 30 minutes.

(If you're making individual galettes, lay the pastry out on a lightly floured bench and cut out six 16 cm (6¼ in) discs. Any scraps can be pushed back together and rolled out again. Lay the discs on a lined tray and refrigerate them while you prepare the fruit.)

Slice the peaches in half and de-stone them. Leave six of the halves intact and slice the other six into five slim wedges each. Combine the peach halves and wedges in a bowl with the sprigs of rosemary. In a separate bowl, mix the sugar, vanilla and cinnamon to create a lightly spiced sugar mix. Add the sugar mix to the peaches and toss gently with a spoon so the sugar evenly coats the fruit.

Remove the pastry from the fridge and place it on a baking tray, removing the top layer of baking paper. Lay the slim peach wedges over the base, leaving a 4 cm (1½ in) border around the edge of the pastry, with the thin side of the wedges facing the outer rim of the circle. Fold the 4 cm (1½ in) margin of pastry in towards the centre, over the peach wedges, and crimp the edges together to seal the pastry in place with the peach slices underneath. Place the peach halves over the centre, cut-side up, spacing them out neatly. Chill in the fridge for 30 minutes. While the galette is chilling, preheat the oven to 175°C (350 °F).

Make the egg wash by lightly whisking the egg, milk and salt together. Remove the galette from the fridge, brush the exposed pastry with the egg wash and sprinkle with raw sugar. Bake for 15 minutes . Rotate the tray in the oven and reduce the temperature to 165°C (330°F) and bake for another 10–15 minutes, until the pastry is golden brown. Set aside to cool for 10–15 minutes before serving.

Apple and buckwheat pie

We are blessed to live in a climate that grows great apples, and to have access to wonderful farmers' markets where we can meet the people who grow them and express our thanks. John Howell grows a wonderful range of apples on his multi-generation farm in Wandin North, bringing different varieties to market as the weather changes. We like a crisp, tart eating apple here – Granny Smith, Stewart's Seedling, Fuji or Braeburn are good.

SEASONS ALTERED

If you, like us, have the privilege to access local fruit from a good grower, you will find this recipe alters itself as time marches on. Apples of different varieties ripen at different times, and bring their individual characteristics to your bake. It's like a single-ingredient education in seasonal variation.

If your apples are on the sweeter side, adjust the sugar accordingly, reducing the amount by about 10 g (¼ oz).

Serves 8–10

8–10 medium sized apples, peeled, cored and sliced
80 g (2¾ oz) raw (demerara) sugar
50 g (1¾ oz) soft brown sugar
20 g (¾ oz) cornflour (cornstarch)
grated zest and juice of 2 lemons
1 teaspoon ground cinnamon
½ teaspoon freshly grated nutmeg
½ teaspoon ground ginger
1 vanilla bean, seeds scraped (or 1 teaspoon vanilla paste)
1 teaspoon fine sea salt
1 quantity Flaky buckwheat pastry (page 26), cut into two equal pieces
raw (demerara) sugar, for sprinkling

Egg wash

1 egg
splash of full-cream (whole) milk
pinch of fine sea salt

Cut the apples into 5 mm (¼ in) thick slices and put them in a large saucepan along with the sugars, cornflour, lemon zest and juice, spices, vanilla and salt. Stir to mix well, then cook over a low–medium heat for 8–10 minutes, stirring occasionally with a wooden spoon, until the apples are tender. Set aside to cool.

Grease a tart case 26 cm (10¼ in) in diameter and 5 cm (2 in) deep. Roll one piece of the pastry into a disc 3–4 mm (⅛–¼ in) thick. Lay it over the tart case and use your thumbs to press the pastry into the corners all the way around, leaving a little overhanging at the edges to account for shrinkage. Roll the other piece of pastry out until it's 3–4 mm (⅛–¼ in) thick, and cut it into strips 2 cm (¾ in) wide.

Make the egg wash by lightly whisking the egg, milk and salt together. Transfer your cooled apple filling into the tart case, and use the pastry strips to create a lattice pattern over the top of the fruit. Press the lattice strips into the tart base at the edges, or turn the edges up and crimp them together, and lightly brush the exposed pastry with egg wash. Sprinkle generously with raw sugar, then put your prepared pie in the fridge to rest for 30 minutes. Preheat the oven to 180°C (360°F).

Bake for 1 hour until the pastry is golden all over. Check the pie after 45 minutes and rotate it in the oven. If at that point you find your pastry is darkening too quickly around the edges, carefully place a few strips of foil over the pastry around the circumference, and continue to bake until the centre is more golden in appearance.

Once baked, cool for 10 minutes before serving. This is incredible with vanilla-bean ice cream or clotted cream.

Flourless chocolate cake

This dark, springy chocolate cake is easy to eat and useful for any occasion. The texture is light and mousse-like, making it dangerously hard to stop at just one slice. It also happens to be gluten and nut free. This flourless chocolate cake is more than just a dessert; it's an experience, a journey into the world of chocolate that's simply irresistible.

SEASONS ALTERED

Add another element by folding dried raspberries or cherries into the mixture before pouring it into the tin. Chocolate and red fruits are a match made in heaven, and the bursts of tart, chewy fruit as you eat the cake are just wonderful.

Serves 8–10

250 g (9 oz) dark chocolate, at least 60% cacao

60 g (2 oz) cocoa powder

120 g (4½ oz) full-cream (whole) milk

1 tablespoon lemon juice

170 g (6 oz) eggs, at room temperature

160 g (5½ oz) caster (superfine) sugar

120 g (4½ oz) double (heavy) cream

150 g (5½ oz) egg whites, at room temperature

cocoa powder, for dusting

double (heavy) cream, to serve

Preheat the oven to 150°C (300°F). Grease and line a 23 cm (9 in) round cake tin.

Put the chocolate in a bowl and sit it over a saucepan with a little water in the bottom, ensuring the water doesn't touch the bowl. Place over a medium heat to melt the chocolate. Once the chocolate has melted, whisk in the cocoa powder.

Gently bring the milk to a simmer in a small saucepan, then add to the chocolate mixture and whisk it in. Add the lemon juice and whisk until well combined, then transfer to a large mixing bowl and set aside.

In a stand mixer, whisk the eggs and 100 g (3½ oz) of the caster sugar on a medium speed for about 10 minutes until pale and fluffy.

In a separate bowl, whisk the cream until soft peaks form, then refrigerate while you prepare the egg whites.

Whisk the egg whites and remaining sugar on a low–medium speed to form stiff peaks. Once this is done you are ready to bring it all together.

Use a spatula to fold the egg yolk mixture into the chocolate mixture, in two additions. Next, fold in the whipped cream, and then finally the meringue. Gently fold it through until just combined, then pour the mixture into your prepared tin and put it on the top shelf in the oven.

Bake for 40–50 minutes until the cake has risen. There will be cracks in the surface, and if you gently shake it the cake will have a full wobble. Leave to cool on a wire rack for about 1 hour. Lightly dust the top with cocoa powder and serve with cream.

Burnt orange Basque cheesecake

Originating from the coastal Spanish town of San Sebastian, a Basque cheesecake typically consists of a combination of cream, sugar and eggs. It differs from other baked cheesecakes as it doesn't have a crust. Instead, it is baked at a high temperature to give its signature 'burnt' surface, which also holds it together. This recipe comes from our great friend Raul Cintero Matas, who also hails from San Sebastian and is a wonderful pastry chef.

Cheese is best served at room temperature and the same goes for cheesecake. If you refrigerate the cake before serving, remove it from the fridge an hour beforehand to bring it up to temperature.

SEASONS ALTERED

This cake is wonderful served with berries or another slightly tart fruit. Poached rhubarb is ideal in winter; try raspberries or blackberries in summer.

Serves 8–10

1 kg (2 lb 3 oz) cream cheese, at room temperature, roughly chopped

400 g (14 oz) raw caster (superfine) sugar

7 medium eggs, at room temperature

40 g (1½ oz) plain (all-purpose) flour

½ teaspoon fine sea salt

1 vanilla bean, seeds scraped (or 1 teaspoon vanilla paste)

grated zest of 1 orange

400 g (14 oz) double (heavy) cream

Preheat the oven to 200°C (390°F). Grease a 23 cm (9 in) loose-bottomed or springform cake tin. Line the rim with baking paper that extends at least 5 cm (2 in) above the edge of the tin to allow for the cheesecake to rise during baking. (It will sink again once cooled.)

In the bowl of a stand mixer fitted with the paddle attachment, beat the cream cheese and sugar for 5 minutes on medium speed. With the mixer still running, add the eggs one at a time. In a separate bowl, mix the flour, salt, vanilla and orange zest. Reduce the mixer speed to low and add the flour mixture. Mix until incorporated, then add the cream and mix until smooth, scraping down the side and base of the bowl to ensure everything is well mixed through.

Pour the mixture into the lined cake tin then give the tin a sharp bang on the bench to remove any large air bubbles. Bake for 40 minutes, then rotate the tin in the oven and bake for another 10–15 minutes, until the top is deeply caramelised and puffed up like a soufflé. If you find there isn't much colour, increase the temperature to 220°C (430°F) and bake until the top is an almost slightly singed dark brown. It should have a wobble when you shake the tin. Set aside to cool completely in the tin.

Serve in generous slices on its own or with seasonal fruit of your choice. Store in an airtight container in the fridge for up to 4 days.

Brown butter plum clafoutis

The wow-factor of a clafoutis is inversely proportional to the ease of making one. Just before dinner, make a quick batter, lay some beautiful seasonal fruit into a baking dish and pour the batter over the top. Pop it in the oven while you eat your meal and enjoy a satisfyingly creamy, fruit-based, baked custard pudding to follow. No pastry, no fuss. You can even make the batter in advance and use it straight from the fridge.

SEASONS SHARED

Cherry clafoutis is a late-spring classic – just be sure to tell your guests to mind the pips. Any stone fruit works in summer, and fig clafoutis is for early autumn. Use Poached quinces (page 211) in winter for a fireside dessert.

Serves 4

4 medium-sized blood plums

50 g (1¾ oz) unsalted butter

2 medium eggs, at room temperature

60 g (2 oz) raw (demerara) sugar

50 g (1¾ oz) plain (all-purpose) flour

50 g (1¾ oz) ground almonds

1 vanilla bean, seeds scraped (or 1 teaspoon vanilla paste)

pinch of fine sea salt

300 g (10½ oz) full-cream (whole) milk

unsalted butter, for greasing

vanilla bean ice cream, to serve

Halve the plums and remove the stones. Cut each half into three wedges and set aside.

Melt the butter in a small saucepan over a medium heat, and cook until it starts to foam and gives off a nutty aroma. Remove from the heat and pass it through a fine sieve into a small bowl.

Whisk the eggs and sugar in a medium bowl to combine. Add the flour, ground almonds, vanilla and salt and mix well. Add the milk and butter, and whisk until combined, with no lumps. Rest the mixture in the fridge for 20 minutes, or overnight.

Preheat the oven to 190°C (375°F). Brush four shallow dishes, roughly 15 cm (6 in) in diameter, with butter. Arrange 5–6 wedges of plum in each dish, cut-side up, then pour the batter around the fruit. You should still be able to see the tops of the plums.

Bake for 20–25 minutes until the top is golden and there is a slight wobble in the centre. Leave to cool for 5 minutes, then serve hot with a scoop of your favourite ice cream on top, or simply enjoy the texture of the fruit and baked custard together.

Dark ale pudding with salted caramel sauce

A heart-warming winter pudding, this was on the menu at The Commoner in Fitzroy. There, Jo Corrigan and Matthew Donnelly produced beautifully sourced food, thoughtfully cooked and served with love, before embarking on a tree change. This pudding was always reason enough for a visit. Thankfully, Jo and Matt have kindly shared their recipe so we can continue to enjoy it – and now you can too.

This is a Very British Pudding, all grown up with the deep flavours of a dark ale and salted caramel sauce. This dessert transcends the ordinary with its deep, malty notes and the comforting embrace of a steaming pudding.

SEASONS ALTERED

Use other brews such as stout or porter for a nice variation.

We've used a 240 ml (8 fl oz) pudding mould here. Don't rush out to buy new equipment especially – you can also use a muffin tray for perfectly good puddings.

Serves 6

115 g (4 oz) plain (all-purpose) flour
¼ teaspoon baking powder
1 teaspoon bicarbonate of soda (baking soda)
50 g (1¾ oz) Dutch cocoa powder
115 g (4 oz) unsalted butter, softened
150 g (5½ oz) raw (demerara) sugar
1 vanilla bean, seeds scraped (or 1 teaspoon vanilla paste)
2 large eggs, at room temperature
200 g (7 oz) dark ale
cream, to serve

Salted caramel sauce

200 g (7 oz) raw (demerara) sugar
120 g (4½ oz) double (heavy) cream
60 g (2 oz) unsalted butter
5 g (⅛ oz) fine sea salt

To make the salted caramel sauce, melt the sugar in a heavy-bottomed saucepan over a medium heat. Stir frequently as the sugar melts, and cook it out until you have a deep amber caramel. This can take 10–12 minutes. If the sugar starts to burn before it's caramelised, reduce the heat slightly.

Add the cream to the caramel. Be careful – the caramel may bubble and spit as it meets the cool cream, so pour gently to prevent injury. Stir until the cream is fully incorporated, and then add the butter and sea salt. Continue to stir until the butter has melted and the sauce is smooth. Taste the sauce and adjust the level of salt to your liking. Set aside to cool and thicken.

Once the sauce has reached your desired consistency, transfer it to a glass jar or airtight container. You can use it immediately or refrigerate for future use.

To make the pudding, preheat the oven to 180°C (360°F). Grease 6 × 240 ml (8 fl oz) pudding moulds or a 6-hole muffin tray. Cut a disc of baking paper to fit the base of each mould and place it in the bottom – this will make it much easier to extract the puddings from the moulds once cooked.

Mix the flour, baking powder, bicarbonate of soda and cocoa powder, sifting to mix well.

In a stand mixer fitted with the paddle attachment, cream the butter, sugar and vanilla on medium–high speed for about 10 minutes, until pale and smooth, scraping down the side of the bowl as required to ensure an even mix.

Lightly whisk the eggs in a small bowl. With the mixer still running, add the egg in two or three stages, ensuring each addition is fully incorporated before adding the next. Scrape down the side of the bowl as required.

Turn off the machine and then gradually incorporate the dry mixture, folding it in with a spatula. Mix gently until fully incorporated, then add the dark ale and mix well. It can be useful to use a whisk at this stage to help mix everything together well.

Divide the mixture between your pudding moulds, filling each to just over halfway. Place them in a roasting tray and pour hot water into the bottom of the tray, to reach three-quarters of the way up your moulds. Cover the tray with foil and bake for 1 hour. If you're using a different size mould you may need to adjust the baking time. They're done when they've risen to the height of the moulds and a knife inserted into the centre of one tests clean. Carefully remove your puddings from the bain marie and cool on a wire rack for 10 minutes before demoulding. Slide a small palette knife or thin-tipped knife around the edge of each pudding and gently tip it out.

To serve, place each pudding on a plate and pour caramel sauce over the top, and a dollop of cream.

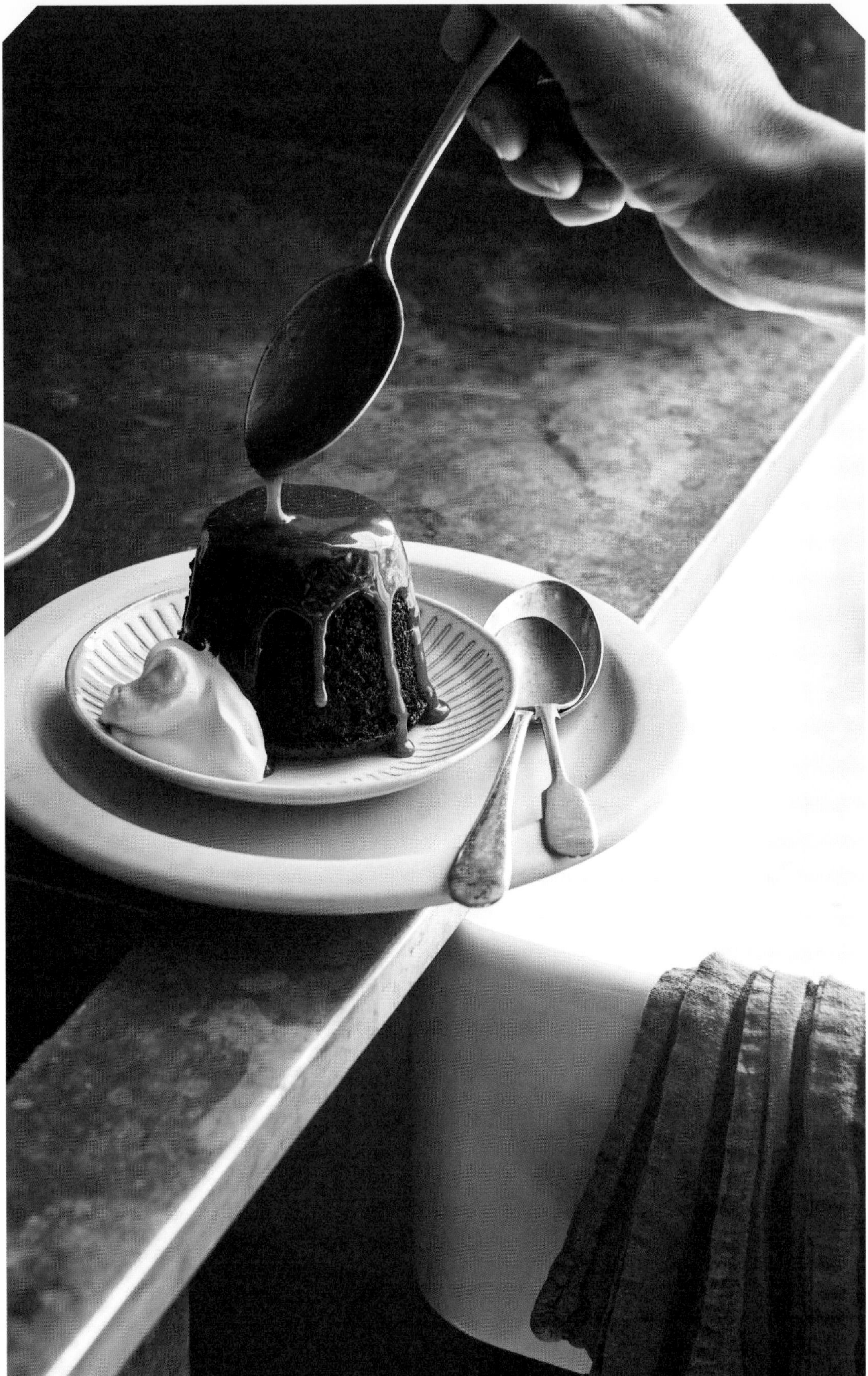

A rum baba is a yeasted cake, soaked in a sweet alcoholic syrup. Served with pillows of softly whipped cream, it's boozy and decadent. This is a gentle entry point to yeasted bakes, an enriched dough with the safety net of a tin for it to rise in – no need to worry about shaping sticky doughs.

You can make the cake and the syrup in advance. A slightly stale baba will really soak and hold the syrup for delicious results. If making the syrup in advance, you will need to reheat it before soaking the sponge. Hold the rum and add it at the last minute so it doesn't burn off as you warm it up. And remember: the better your rum, the better your baba.

SEASONS ALTERED

These may be called rum babas, but feel free to use any spirit you like to make them your own. A non-alcoholic version is also lovely – just omit the rum when making the syrup. It can always be added at the table for those who would like some. Serve with fresh raspberries or blackberries for something different.

We've used a 240 ml (8 fl oz) pudding mould here. Don't rush out to buy new equipment especially – you can also use a muffin tray for perfectly good puddings. Smaller babas are also nice. Whatever size you make, ensure you fill the moulds to just a little over halfway to leave room for the rise.

Serves 6

100 g (3½ oz) full-cream (whole) milk

6 g (⅕ oz) instant dried yeast

180 g (6½ oz) bakers (strong) flour

1 whole egg (60 g/2 oz)

1 egg yolk (18 g/⅔ oz)

12 g (½ oz) dark muscovado sugar

5 g (⅛ oz) fine sea salt

50 g (1¾ oz) unsalted butter, roughly chopped and softened, plus extra for greasing

350 g (12½ oz) double (heavy) cream, whipped to soft peaks, to serve

Syrup

400 g (14 oz) raw (demerara) sugar

500 g (1 lb 2 oz) water

1 vanilla bean, seeds scraped (or 1 teaspoon vanilla paste)

grated zest and juice of 1 orange

200 g (7 oz) dark rum

Warm the milk in a small saucepan over a low heat until the temperature reaches 35°C (95°F). Combine with the yeast and 50 g (1¾ oz) of the flour in the bowl of a stand mixer. Use a fork or your hand to stir well, then set aside for 15 minutes, until there are signs of life. The batter will start to foam and smell a bit yeasty.

Add the remaining flour along with the whole egg and yolk, sugar and salt, and beat using the dough hook for about 4 minutes on medium speed. Scrape down the side of the bowl with a spatula, then add the butter in two additions. Mix on a medium–high speed for another 4 minutes until fully incorporated. Scrape down the sides of the bowl and cover with a damp tea towel, then rest in a warm place for 45 minutes until the mixture has risen by a third.

While the batter is proving, grease 6 × 240 ml (8 fl oz) pudding moulds or a 6-hole muffin tray. Cut a disc of baking paper to fit the base of each mould and place it in the bottom – this will make it easier to extract the puddings from the moulds later on.

Divide the mixture between your pudding moulds, filling each to just over halfway. Wet your fingers and tap the top of the batter to even it out in the mould. Leave to prove in a warm place for 1 hour, or until the batter reaches the top of the mould. Towards the end of the prove, preheat the oven to 180°C (360°F).

Bake for 10 minutes, then turn the tray and bake for another 3–4 minutes until the babas are a deep golden colour on top. Cool for a couple of minutes in the moulds, then tip onto a cooling rack.

To make the syrup, bring the sugar, water, vanilla, orange zest and juice to a simmer in a saucepan, stirring to dissolve the sugar. Simmer for 5 minutes then remove from the heat, add the rum and set aside.

Place your babas in a large, deep mixing bowl and pour the warm syrup over the top. Leave them to stand in the syrup for up to 30 minutes with a plate or other weight on top to keep them submerged, turning occasionally to ensure an even soak.

To serve, drain the excess syrup and place each baba on a plate. Serve with whipped cream alongside a bottle of rum, so your guests can doctor their pudding to their tastes.

Seasons marked

Ritual bakes to mark
your calendar

Pages 165–89

To say that food supports life is obvious. Our bodies need to be nourished to keep us active and thriving, and we're constantly told about the importance of eating well. But our spirit is not separate from our body. Each time we sit at a beautifully laid table to eat with people we love, we create memories and connections that are equally important to our wellbeing. The recipes in this chapter relate to specific times of the year and particular rituals. Descending, as we both do, from Anglo–Christian cultures, many of them relate to the liturgical year.

Christmas features heavily here, both with traditional bakes and others that we've co-opted into our own traditions. Growing up in Australia, Pippa always ate cherries at Christmas time, and their vibrant colour is entirely appropriate for the season. Good cherries are a valuable crop, and the cherry pie can be seen as an extravagance befitting the festive season. It's so delicious, we encourage you to make it at least once.

Summer pudding is another non-traditional dish that we've absorbed into our Christmas repertoire. We get excited when berries are back after the hungry gap, and summer pudding is a perfect excuse to gorge on them. It also provides a weather-appropriate dessert for a celebration that somehow doesn't quite make sense in a warm climate. Sherry trifle is not strictly traditional but often features on the Christmas table in England, where Michael enjoyed his childhood Christmases. Quinces preserved in autumn are emboldened with Pedro Ximénez, and finished with hazelnuts and cacao nibs for texture.

Mince pies, Christmas pudding and Christmas cake, the traditional stalwarts of the season, are all here, rich with dried fruit soaked in alcohol. Choose the best fruit you can find – it really will make all the difference. The same goes for your hot cross buns. Fresh from the oven, these boldly spiced, yeasted buns are so delicious.

Nougat and gingerbread make excellent gifts. Galette des Rois is a simple French bake to celebrate the Epiphany. Featuring delicate puff pastry and rich almond frangipane, a small slice is the perfect end to a festive season of delicious indulgence.

This chapter features several slow makes, requiring some manual labour, multiple elements or maturing over many months. The best approach is to share the load, working side by side with someone you enjoy spending time with. Drink tea and chat while you pit your cherries or peel your quinces. Make a ritual of stirring your fruit mince or feeding your Christmas cake, and feed your soul as you go.

Cherry and rye pie

Cherries herald the coming of Christmas in Australia. The lead-up to year's end can feel hectic, and the making of this pie is an antidote to the frenetic pace of the season. It holds the lesson that good things take time, and it will taste better if you lean into that.

Pitting a kilo of cherries is a task best shared in a relaxed way, creating space for conversation to unfold, possibly with some test cricket on in the background. Be sure to taste as you work – who can resist fresh cherries? If your cherries are a little tart, add another 10 g (¼ oz) of sugar. Very sweet cherries will benefit from an extra squeeze of lemon juice.

You can use frozen pitted cherries here. Defrost them in a sieve over a bowl to collect the juice as they thaw. Reduce the juice slightly in a pan over a medium heat to concentrate the flavour before adding it back to the cherries.

SEASONS ALTERED

Use spelt in place of rye flour for a softer, nuttier flavour in the pastry. Any wholegrain flour will do nicely.

Serves 8–10

800 g (1 lb 12 oz) fresh pitted cherries (1 kg/2 lb 3 oz whole unpitted)

140 g (5 oz) raw cane sugar

28 g (1 oz) cornflour (cornstarch)

1 vanilla bean, seeds scraped (or 1 teaspoon vanilla paste)

1 tablespoon lemon juice

grated zest of 1 lemon

1 quantity Whole rye flaky pastry (page 26)

20 g (¾ oz) unsalted butter, cut into 1 cm (½ in) dice

raw (demerara) sugar, to sprinkle

clotted cream, vanilla ice cream or mascarpone (page 127) to serve

Egg wash

1 egg

splash of full-cream (whole) milk

pinch of fine sea salt

Put the pitted cherries in a bowl with the sugar, cornflour, vanilla, lemon juice and zest. Stir gently to combine well, then set aside to macerate for a couple of hours, or overnight.

Meanwhile, prepare your rested pastry. Grease a 23 cm (9 in) pie dish. Divide the pastry in half and roll one piece out into a circle 3 mm (⅛ in) thick – this is for the bottom of your pie. We're not blind baking it, so you don't want it to be thick (thick pastry equals undercooked pastry, and nobody wants that).

Gently lay your pastry circle over the pie dish and use your thumb to press it into the corners. Leave any overhang for now, to allow for shrinkage. Transfer your lined dish to the fridge and turn your attention to the other piece of pastry.

Roll the second piece of pastry out to 4 mm (¼ in) thick and cut strips 5 cm (2 in) wide for the lattice top. You will need differing lengths – longer ones for the middle, shorter for the edges. Lay the strips on a tray and pop it in the fridge.

When you're ready to finish building the pie, preheat the oven to 190°C (375°F). If you have a pizza stone, it's a good idea to put it in the oven now, as the extra heat will help to bake the base. Make the egg wash by lightly whisking the egg, milk and salt together.

Strain your cherries and put the liquid in a small, heavy-based saucepan. Reduce over a medium heat until thick and jammy. Put the cherries in the pie dish, pour over the thickened juice and scatter the butter cubes over the top. Arrange the pastry strips into a closed lattice over the pie, weaving as you go. Gently press the edges together to seal the pie, or pinch the pastry into a crimped pattern, and gently trim any overhanging pieces (keep these for another use).

Brush the top of the pastry with egg wash and sprinkle the lattice strips with raw sugar. Bake for 20 minutes, then reduce the heat to 180°C (360°F) and bake for another 20–30 minutes, until your pastry is lovely and golden. If the pastry is getting dark around the edges while the middle is still underbaked, gently fold strips of aluminium foil over the edges to protect them while the rest bakes through.

Cool for 10 minutes before serving with clotted cream, vanilla ice cream or mascarpone.

Galette des rois

This galette is served in France at the Fête des Rois, the celebration of the epiphany in the Christian calendar, when the three kings visited baby Jesus. Custom holds that the person who discovers the *fève* inside is crowned king or queen for the evening. It's simple to make, rich and tasty, and looks beautiful, with the curved marks in flaky golden puff pastry – three very good reasons to make it, whether or not you adhere to the origin story.

The *fève* is a small trinket found inside the cake. We've used a whole almond, but you could also use a dried bean, coin or ornament.

SEASONS ALTERED

Berry or plum jam would work well instead of the apricot jam, and would provide a beautiful contrast of colour.

Serves 4–6

400 g (14 oz) Puff pastry (page 30)

50 g (1¾ oz) Apricot and amaretto jam (page 204)

300 g (10½ oz) Almond frangipane (page 39)

1 whole almond, or other *fève* (optional)

Egg wash

1 egg

splash of full-cream (whole) milk

pinch of fine sea salt

Roll the puff pastry into a rectangle roughly 24 × 45 cm (9½ × 17¾ in), and 3 mm (⅛ in) thick. Cut out one disc 22 cm (8¾ in) in diameter, and another 20 cm (8 in) in diameter. If you don't have a cutter for precision, use plates or bowls to get roughly the same sizes. Refrigerate for 1 hour.

Line a baking tray with baking paper. Make the egg wash by lightly whisking the egg, milk and salt together.

Place the smaller of the two pastry discs on the baking tray, spoon the jam onto it and spread it across the surface, leaving a 2 cm (¾ in) border around the edge. Pipe or spoon the frangipane into an even layer over the jam. Place the *fève* on top, to be discovered by the lucky monarch later.

Pierce the very centre of the larger pastry disc. With a small mixing bowl as your guide, use the back of a knife to score a curve from the middle to the edge of the disc. Repeat this pattern all the way around, leaving a 2 cm (¾ in) gap between each score.

Lightly brush the 2 cm (¾ in) exposed border on the smaller pastry piece with egg wash, and carefully drape the larger one neatly over it with the scoring visible on top. Press the edges together with your thumb to seal your galette, gently expelling air from inside as you go. Crimp the edges for decorative effect, or use the back of a knife to push into the pastry about 1 cm towards the centre all around the galette pastry. Lightly brush the top with egg wash and then refrigerate for at least 20 minutes.

Preheat the oven to 180°C (360°F). Place the tray on the top shelf and bake for 30 minutes, then reduce the heat to 160°C (320°F), rotate the tray and bake for another 20–25 minutes, until golden and flaky. Cool on the tray for 5–10 minutes before serving. Store in an airtight container for up to 4 days.

Summer pudding

It would be remiss to omit this totem of the British summer when compiling our favourite seasonal recipes. Fresh berries picked on meandering country walks, lifted with the aroma of elderflower and held in slices of soft honey milk bread; this pudding encapsulates the best of midsummer eating. We often have summer pudding on our Christmas table in Australia, and heartily recommend creating some kind of annual ritual involving this dish, just to remind yourself how good it is.

Make the honey milk loaf at least one day ahead, and leave it out to stale a little so it soaks up all the juices. Assemble the pudding the day before serving.

SEASONS ALTERED

As the days start to draw in and the torrent of summer's berries subsides, rhubarb is a mainstay, the first apples ripen and blackberries are abundant. Lightly stew some rhubarb and diced apple over a low heat with a little sugar. Combine in a bowl with fresh blackberries and you have yourself an Autumn pudding. Use 1 kg (2 lb 3 oz) of fruit in total, and proceed with the recipe as below.

Verbena lemonade makes an aromatic alternative to elderflower, equally fragrant and delicious.

Serves 6–8

250 g (9 oz) strawberries, hulled and halved

250 g (9 oz) raspberries

250 g (9 oz) blueberries

250 g (9 oz) blackberries

100 g (3½ oz) raw (demerara) sugar

grated zest and juice of 1 lemon

50 g (1¾ oz) Elderflower cordial (page 197) or 5 fresh elderflower heads

grated zest and juice of 1 lemon

Milk and honey loaf

400 g (14 oz) bakers (strong) flour

70 g (2½ oz) honey

6 g (⅛ oz) fine sea salt

1 egg, at room temperature

240 g (8½ oz) full-cream (whole) milk

8 g (¼ oz) instant dried yeast

80 g (2¾ oz) unsalted butter, roughly chopped and softened

Egg wash (optional)

1 egg

splash of full-cream (whole) milk

pinch of fine sea salt

To make the milk and honey loaf, combine the flour, honey, salt, egg, milk and yeast in the mixing bowl of a stand mixer fitted with the dough hook. Mix on a low speed for 5 minutes to incorporate the ingredients, stopping occasionally to scrape down the side of the bowl.

Check the consistency; it should be like slightly sticky playdough. Increase the speed to medium and mix for a further 5 minutes, then add the butter all at once. Don't worry about overcrowding the bowl – it will all work itself out and mix through.

Continue to mix on a medium speed for another 8 minutes. You may need to stop to scrape down the side of the bowl a few times. Mix until your dough comes away from the side of the bowl and is velvety and smooth. You should be able to stretch it out without it breaking.

Cover and set aside for an hour, ideally at around 22–24°C (72–75°F). If the weather is too cold, put it in your (cold) oven with a light on and a pan of hot water at the bottom to create warmth and humidity.

After 1 hour, give the dough a fold. To fold, wet or oil your hands and grab a piece of dough on the side of the bowl. Pull and stretch it up over the middle to the other side of the bowl. Repeat this 6–8 times, moving around the edge of the bowl. You can also knead the dough on the benchtop.

Cover once more and set aside at room temperature to prove for another hour or so, until it has risen and when you shake the bowl the dough wobbles a little, and feels light and full of air. Check if it's ready by gently poking the dough. If your fingertip leaves a dent, it's ready, but if the dough springs back quickly, cover again and give it more time.

Once the dough is ready, shape, prove and bake your loaf. Lightly grease a 12 × 25 cm (4¾ × 10 in), 7 cm (2¾ in) deep, straight-sided loaf tin. Tip your fully proved dough onto a lightly floured kitchen bench and divide it into three equal pieces, about 260 g (9 oz) each.

You now need to shape each piece of dough into a tight ball. Take one piece and knock out any large bubbles, then fold the outside edges into the middle, and turn it over so the seam is underneath. Place your dominant hand over the dough and push it down as you move your hand in a circular motion, rotating the dough in your palm.

You may find it easier to cup both hands around the dough. Applying pressure as you shape the pieces builds strength in the dough and makes it more taut. This process should take about 30 seconds. Repeat with the remaining two pieces. Put the three balls in the tin, smooth side up, then cover and set aside to prove, ideally at 22–24°C (72-75°F) for 1–1½ hours.

After 1 hour, preheat the oven to 170°C (340°F). If your dough is ready but your oven is not quite up to temperature, put the tin in the fridge until you are ready to bake.

Make the egg wash, if using, by lightly whisking the egg, milk and salt together. Just before baking, lightly brush the top with egg wash or spray it with water. Bake on the top shelf of the oven for 25–30 minutes, turning the tin halfway through to ensure an even bake. To test if the loaf is ready, remove it from the tin and tap the bottom; if it sounds hollow it's ready. Cool in the tin on a wire rack.

When you're ready to assemble your pudding, combine the berries in a colander and give them a rinse, then drain well. Transfer to a large saucepan and add the sugar, lemon zest and juice, and cordial or elderflower heads. Cook over a low–medium heat for 5 minutes, stirring occasionally to dissolve the sugar, until the berries start to release their juices. Remove from the heat and set aside to cool. Once cool, remove the flower heads (if using) and strain the berries through a fine sieve to separate the fruit from the berry juices.

Lightly grease a 1-litre (34 fl oz) pudding bowl, and line it with plastic wrap or baking paper.

Cut the ends off the milk and honey loaf and slice it into 1 cm (½ in) thick slices. Brush each slice with the berry juices, and use them to line the bowl. Start by placing one slice at the bottom of the bowl to create a base, and then overlap slices to line the inside of the bowl, leaving a few slices aside for the top. Fill the bowl with the fruit and pour some of the juices over the top, until it looks sodden. Seal the fruit inside under 2–3 slices of bread then pour more syrup over the top, reserving some to serve alongside the pudding.

Top the pudding with a small plate or saucer, weighted down with a can or other small heavy object. Refrigerate overnight to press, and for the bread to soak up all those berry good juices.

To serve, remove the weight and plate, then invert a serving plate over the top of the bowl. Flip everything over so the plate is underneath the pudding, and carefully lift the bowl off the top. Remove the lining and behold your glorious summer pudding. Slice the pudding and serve in bowls, with some double cream and the remaining berry juices.

Quince and hazelnut sherry trifle

Like many traditional British puddings, trifle has been ruined for many by memories of school dinners: gluggy custard, cloyingly sweet tinned fruit, fluorescent jelly and soggy sponge. But a fine version is no trifling thing. It's a celebration of seasonal fruit at its best, ably supported by flavoursome sponge, delicate jelly and lashings of luscious cream. Sherry makes it Christmas, Pedro Ximénex being a bit of a twist.

There are quite a few elements to combine here. But preparing it ahead of time allows all the flavours to marry, so do the work over a few days to minimise the overwhelm, and then enjoy the fun of putting it all together the day before you serve it.

If you have a round trifle bowl, around 20 cm (8 in) diameter, you can use the round sponge as the base and layer the fruit, custard and cream on top. If not, just cut the sponge to fit the base of your bowl. Don't worry – your cake will be well hidden by jelly, fruit and custard.

SEASONS ALTERED

Combining many elements gives you lots of creative freedom. Use berries or cherries instead of quince, or gently poached rhubarb and pistachio.

Serves 8–10

½ quantity Brown butter sponge (page 52), baked in a 20 cm (8 in) round tin

30 g (1 oz) toasted hazelnuts, roughly chopped

20 g (¾ oz) cacao nibs

Custard

500 g (1 lb 2 oz) double (heavy) cream

75 g (2¾ oz) full-cream (whole) milk

1 teaspoon ground cinnamon

grated zest of 1 orange

1 vanilla bean, seeds scraped, pod reserved (or paste)

6 egg yolks, at room temperature

60 g (2 oz) raw (demerara) sugar

Jelly

500 g (1 lb 2oz) Poached quinces, in syrup (page 211)

2 teaspoons gelatine powder

100 g (3½ oz) Pedro Ximénez or sweet sherry

Whipped cream topping

250 g (9 oz) double (heavy) cream

Make the sponge first, then leave it for a day or so to stale a little bit. A stale sponge will absorb more liquid. Because you're doing a half recipe, the bake time will be reduced. Check the sponge after 15 minutes in the oven, and bake just until light golden brown.

To make the custard, combine the cream, milk, cinnamon, orange zest, and vanilla seeds and pod in a heavy based saucepan. Bring the mixture to a simmer over a medium heat. Remove from the heat and set aside to infuse for a few minutes, then strain it into a bowl and discard the solids.

Lightly whisk the egg yolks and sugar together in a large bowl. Gradually add the warm cream mixture, a little at a time, gently stirring until well combined and smooth. Pour into a clean saucepan and cook over a low–medium heat, stirring regularly, until the mixture reaches 82°C (180°F) or until it coats the back of a spoon. Strain into a bowl, cover with baking paper touching the surface and refrigerate overnight.

To make the jelly, strain the quinces, reserving the syrup. Combine 100 g (3½ oz) quince syrup with the gelatine powder and leave to bloom for 5–10 minutes. Gently heat another 300 g (10½ oz) of syrup with the Pedro Ximénez, add the syrup and gelatine bloom, and whisk well. Set aside to cool to room temperature, and then refrigerate if not using immediately. Place any remaining quince syrup in a saucepan over a medium heat, and reduce to the consistency of runny honey. Refrigerate until you're ready to assemble your trifle.

To assemble, trim the sponge to fit the base of your trifle bowl then sit it in the bottom of the bowl. Using a skewer or sharp knife, make holes in the surface of the sponge to allow the jelly to soak into the sponge. You can help it along by pouring half of the jelly onto the sponge and then using the skewer to guide it into place. Pour the rest of the jelly on top and then spoon in the custard, spreading it evenly across the surface. Lay the poached quince over that, ensuring it's placed in an even layer right to the edges.

Whisk the cream to firm peaks, and then use a spatula or large spoon to dollop it over the top of your quinces. Sprinkle the hazelnuts and cacao nibs over the cream, and finish with a drizzle of the reduced quince syrup. Refrigerate overnight to set.

The next day, serve the trifle in bowls. Take care to give each person a full cross section of the trifle to ensure they get all the elements.

Mince pie creation has become something of a competitive sport among Melbourne bakeries, a little like the hot cross bun frenzy of Easter. Each December, people go from one bakery to the next, compiling their very own top tens. It's taken us a while to let go of that pressure, to relax and enjoy the making of these special little pies that make the holiday season that little bit sweeter.

Make the mince at least two weeks before you make your mince pies. It will last almost indefinitely at room temperature in sterilised jars, developing more in flavour the longer it sits. We make it each year around Christmas time, always working a year ahead. So we'll use last year's mince for this year's mince pies, and make another batch for next year.

Makes 12
(with fruit mince to spare)

Fruit mince

3 Beurre Bosc pears, peeled, cored and diced

4 Granny Smith apples, peeled, cored and diced

185 g (6½ oz) fresh beef suet, minced

330 g (11½ oz) raisins

330 g (11½ oz) currants

330 g (11½ oz) sultanas

90 g (3 oz) Candied mixed peel (page 215), chopped

330 g (11½ oz) soft dark brown sugar

grated zest and juice of 1 orange

grated zest and juice of 2 lemons

3 teaspoons ground mixed spice

1 teaspoon ground allspice

½ teaspoon freshly grated nutmeg

1 teaspoon ground cinnamon

75 g (2¾ oz) slivered almonds

100 g (3½ oz) Armagnac

100 g (3½ oz) Pedro Ximénez

Rich shortcrust pastry

240 g (8½ oz) plain (all-purpose) flour

¾ teaspoon baking powder

90 g (3 oz) caster (superfine) sugar

140 g (5 oz) unsalted butter, chilled, diced

100 g (3½ oz) full-fat cream cheese

60 g (2 oz) ground almonds

1 egg yolk

full cream (whole) milk, if needed

raw (demerara) sugar, to finish

Egg wash

1 egg

splash of full-cream (whole) milk

pinch of fine sea salt

To make the fruit mince, combine all the ingredients except the alcohols in a container with a lid. Mix well and leave in a cool dark place (not the fridge) for 2 days, stirring 2–3 times a day to help macerate the fruit.

On the third day, preheat the oven to 140°C (285°F). Transfer the mixture to a large roasting tray, cover with foil, and bake for around 3 hours, stirring occasionally, until the suet has melted and the mixture is dark and bubbling. Remove from the oven and leave to cool, stirring every 10 minutes to make sure the fruit is coated in suet. Once the mixture is cool, stir through the Armagnac and Pedro Ximénez then spoon into sterilised jars and seal. If you're not storing the fruit mince in sterilised jars, it will also last in an airtight container in the fridge.

To make the pastry, combine the flour, baking powder and sugar in a bowl. Add the diced butter and rub it in until you can see no lumps. Add the cream cheese, ground almonds and egg yolk and rub in until you have a smooth dough (adding a little milk, if necessary). Press the pastry into a disc, cover, and chill for 30 minutes before rolling out to approximately ½ cm (¼ in) thick. Cut discs 8 cm (3¼ in) and 10 cm (4 in) in diameter for the lids and bases, respectively, re-rolling the scraps and cutting again until you have twelve of each size.

Preheat the oven to 190°C (375°F). Make the egg wash by lightly whisking the egg, milk and salt together.

To assemble the pies, lightly butter the cups of a 12-hole muffin tray and line each with one of the larger pastry discs. Fill each hole three-quarters full with fruit mince (roughly 60–80 g/2–2¾ oz per hole) and brush the rim of the pastry with a little water. Place a small pastry disc on top and pinch the edges to seal. Cut a hole in the centre of each pie to allow steam to escape. Brush with egg wash and sprinkle with demerara sugar.

Bake for around 20 minutes, until the pastry is golden brown and the filling is starting to bubble through. Remove from the oven and leave to cool before carefully twisting and easing the pies from the tin. Be careful not to remove the pies from the tin too early, as they'll likely fall apart if they're still hot.

Christmas cake

This is a traditional Christmas recipe that is baked several months ahead and then fed weekly with brandy, to preserve it and develop the flavour. Each week the anticipation builds with the remembrance of last year's Christmas, and the hope (and slight anxiety) that this year's cake will measure up.

This cake is inspired by one Michael first made back in 2004 at the very first Bourke Street Bakery in Sydney's Surry Hills. There, Paul Allam and David McGuinness started their journey, serving up their magic to a devoted following, eventually going on to open multiple stores and cement Bourke Street as a Sydney icon. This recipe has stayed in our family, evolving ever since, and we just love it.

Start soaking the fruit by early September, and make the cake towards the end of the month or early in October. Once baked, douse it with brandy once a week until a week before Christmas. Ideally you will feed the cake for 10 weeks before resting it for at least one to allow the alcohol to settle.

SEASONS ALTERED

In Australia, macadamias are a lovely option to try instead of pistachios and almonds. Hazelnuts go beautifully with the citrus peel and chocolate. Don't limit yourself – changing the nuts is a fabulous way to make this cake your own.

Serves 10–12

Fruit soak

20 g (¾ oz) water

20 g (¾ oz) caster (superfine) sugar

35 g (1¼ oz) brandy

35 g (1¼ oz) Pedro Ximénez

40 g (1½ oz) sultanas

35 g (1¼ oz) currants

70 g (2½ oz) raisins

60 g (2 oz) dried figs, quartered

35 g (1¼ oz) prunes, pitted and quartered

35 g (1¼ oz) dates, pitted and halved

25 g (1 oz) mixed peel
(see Candied mixed peel, page 215)

To make the fruit soak, heat the water, sugar, brandy and Pedro Ximénez in a small saucepan over a medium heat, stirring constantly until the sugar has dissolved. Combine all the other ingredients in a large container with a lid, then pour over the liquid and stir well until all the ingredients are thoroughly combined. Leave the fruit to soak, covered, at room temperature for at least 1 week and up to 2 months. Stir the mixture through occasionally for the first few days to thoroughly distribute the liquid – you want it soaked through the fruit, not settled at the bottom of the container. The longer you leave it, the more the flavour will develop.

To make the cake, preheat the oven to 160°C (280°F). Lightly grease a 15 cm (6 in) round cake tin and line it with baking paper. In a stand mixer fitted with the paddle attachment, gently cream the butter and sugar together until smooth. Add the honey and continue to beat for another 2–3 minutes, until fully incorporated.

Gradually add the eggs in three batches, ensuring that each addition is fully incorporated before adding the next. Work very slowly to ensure that the mixture doesn't curdle at this stage; if you notice it starting to split, add a small amount of plain (all-purpose) flour to bring it back together, but don't worry too much. It will all come together. Continue to beat for about 10 minutes, until pale and light. Meanwhile, combine the flour, almond and spices in a separate bowl and mix well.

Take the bowl off the stand mixer and use a spatula to fold in the flour mixture until just combined. Fold the fruit soak, treacle and marmalade through the mixture. Finally, add the chopped almonds, pistachios and chocolate and mix until combined and evenly distributed. It will become a thick, heavy cake batter.

Transfer the batter into the tin, then wet your hands and gently flatten the top for a nice finish and an even bake. Bake uncovered for 50 minutes, then loosely cover the top with a piece of foil, rotating the tin as you return it to the oven, and bake for another 30 minutes, until the cake is firm to touch and a skewer inserted into the middle comes out clean.

Cake batter

90 g (3 oz) unsalted butter

85 g (3 oz) soft brown sugar

20 g (¾ oz) honey

2 medium eggs, lightly beaten,
   at room temperature

60 g (2 oz) plain (all-purpose) flour

15 g (½ oz) ground almonds

1 teaspoon ground cinnamon

½ teaspoon freshly grated nutmeg

¼ teaspoon ground allspice

¼ teaspoon ground clove

¼ teaspoon ground ginger

20 g (¾ oz) treacle (use honey
   if unavailable)

40 g (1½ oz) Seville orange
   marmalade (page 207)

15 g (½ oz) almonds,
   roughly chopped

15 g (½ oz) pistachios,
   roughly chopped

40 g (1½ oz) dark chocolate,
   roughly chopped (at least
   70% cocoa solids)

brandy, for feeding

Leave to cool in the tin for 30 minutes, then invert the cake onto a wire rack to cool completely. Once cool, lay a sheet of foil large enough to encase the cake on the bench with a sheet of baking paper on top. Place the cake in the middle of the baking paper and bring the edges up over the top to encase the cake, crimping it together to close it on top. Place the wrapped cake in a sealed container and store it in a cool, dark place. After a week, unwrap the cake and use a skewer to make about 20 holes in the top, about two-thirds of the depth of the cake. Brush the top generously with brandy, so that it soaks into the holes and well into the cake – this is called feeding the cake. Feed the cake weekly for 10 weeks, ensuring it is well wrapped in baking paper and foil after each feed. After the last feed, leave the cake for at least a week before eating, although it will last for several months well wrapped in an airtight container, and will continue to mature with age.

Christmas pudding

This pudding has evolved over the years to include ingredients local to where we live now, such as Australia's native macadamias, and the cumquats that grow in abundance in our neighbourhood but are so often left to fall to the ground. Candying the cumquats is like putting money in the bank, the golden jewels sitting pretty on your shelf, ready to be used in your seasonal bakes, or just spread on toast. This is also a great way to meet your neighbours if you don't have a tree. They're usually only too happy to share their harvest and see it used well.

SEASONS ALTERED

If you don't have access to cumquats or haven't thought to candy them in time, use mixed citrus peel or zest instead, for a little zing.

Serves 12–16

125 g (4½ oz) raisins

100 g (3½ oz) sultanas

200 g (7 oz) currants

65 g (2¼ oz) prunes pitted and chopped

65 g (2¼ oz) dates, pitted and chopped

75 g (2¾ oz) apple, peeled, cored, and chopped into 1 cm (½ in) dice

60 g (2 oz) coarse sourdough breadcrumbs (or any kind of coarse breadcrumb)

50 g (1¾ oz) plain (all-purpose) flour

125 g (4½ oz) dark brown sugar

40 g (1 oz) Candied cumquats (see page 216)

30 g (1 oz) slivered almonds, lightly toasted, or chopped toasted whole almonds

30 g (1 oz) macadamia nuts, lightly toasted and roughly chopped

75 g (2¾ oz) suet, coarsely grated

1 teaspoon ground cinnamon

1 teaspoon freshly grated nutmeg

¼ teaspoon ground allspice

¼ teaspoon ground ginger

¼ teaspoon ground clove

2 large eggs

grated zest and juice of 1 orange

grated zest and juice of 1 lemon

15 g (½ oz) treacle (use honey if unavailable)

25 g (1 oz) Pedro Ximénez

75 g (2¾ oz) stout

30 g (1 oz) brandy for feeding, plus 50 g (1¾ oz) extra, to flambé when serving (optional)

Combine the raisins, sultanas, currants, prunes, dates, apple, breadcrumbs, flour, sugar, cumquats, almonds, macadamias, suet and spices in a large mixing bowl and stir well until thoroughly combined.

In a separate bowl, combine the eggs, orange and lemon zest and juice, treacle, Pedro Ximénez, stout and brandy and mix well.

Pour the egg mixture over the fruit mixture and use a large spoon to stir it all through, ensuring the fruit and nuts are well combined and the liquid and spices are evenly distributed. You will have a wet, sloppy mixture. Cover with a lid and leave at room temperature overnight. The breadcrumbs, flour and fruit will soak up the liquids, so by the following day your mixture should be firmer, with only a little free liquid left in the bowl.

Preheat the oven to 160°C (320°F). Lightly grease a 1.2 litre (41 fl oz) pudding bowl, then cut out two discs of baking paper – one the diameter of the base of your pudding bowl, and one the diameter of the top. Place the small disc of baking paper at the base of the bowl. Give the pudding mixture a good stir, then pour it into your prepared bowl. Place the large disc of baking paper over the top, then cover the top of the pudding bowl in several layers of foil, tying it tightly in place with a piece of string.

Fill and boil the kettle. Place the pudding bowl in a large, deep saucepan that will contain the bowl. Pour boiling water around the bowl, up to three-quarters of its height. Put the lid on the saucepan or cover well with foil and cook in the oven for 4 hours. Check the water from time to time and top up if necessary to ensure the water level is maintained.

Remove the pudding from the oven, leaving the bowl in the saucepan. Set aside until completely cool.

Remove the bowl from the pan. Store it in a container in a cool, dark place for up to a year. Every month, uncover the pudding, pierce it a few times with a skewer and sprinkle 20-30 g of brandy over the top, then cover it before storing again. This will keep the pudding moist and add to the final flavour.

On Christmas Day, cover the top with several layers of foil and tie it with string, as you did when it was first cooked. Gently steam the pudding in a steamer basket or saucepan, immersed in boiling water again, for 1 hour, until warmed through. To serve, turn the pudding onto a plate, pour over the extra brandy and set the pudding alight. Serve with your favourite accompaniment: custard, clotted cream or brandy butter.

Chocolate and almond nougat

There is a special magic in the way that egg whites, when whipped with sugar, transform so completely into soft, cloudy peaks, forming a base for many delightful confections. Even after many years of baking, the sight still holds fascination and wonder. Nougat is one of our favourite ways to use up egg whites. It makes a fabulous holiday season gift or petit four.

You will need to work quickly once the sugar heats up. Read the recipe thoroughly before you begin, then weigh up all the ingredients and have them ready. Once you start, it's go! go!! go!!!

SEASONS ALTERED

Using different nuts completely changes the end result. Peanuts create a nougat reminiscent of a Snickers bar. Use hazelnuts for a better-than-Nutella result. Pistachio and chocolate is a long-time favourite, the bright green nuts studding the nougat like jewels. Beautiful.

Makes 20–30

rice paper, for lining your nougat
500 g (1 lb 2 oz) almonds
625 g (1 lb 6 oz) dark chocolate, at least 70% cocoa, roughly chopped
625 g (1 lb 6 oz) raw (demerara) sugar
125 g (4½ oz) water
650 g (1 lb 7 oz) honey
120 g (4½ oz) egg white

Preheat the oven to 160°C (320°F).

Cut two sheets of rice paper to fit the base of a 20 × 30 cm (8 × 12 in) baking tin. Lightly spray or rub oil around the sides of your tin, then line the bottom with one sheet of the rice paper, shiny side up. Set the other sheet aside – you'll use this later to line the top of your nougat.

Put the almonds in a roasting tray and into the oven for 10 minutes, until lightly toasted. Turn off the oven and leave the tray inside to keep the nuts warm while you prepare the mixture.

Put the chocolate in a bowl over a saucepan with hot water in the bottom, ensuring the water does not touch the bowl. Melt the chocolate over a low heat, then keep it warm, taking care not to overheat the chocolate.

Combine the sugar and water in a large saucepan – you need plenty of space for it to expand as it heats up. Place over a low–medium heat and stir to dissolve the sugar. Add the honey and continue to heat steadily, with a sugar thermometer in the saucepan. You're aiming for 130°C (265°F). Once the sugar mixture reaches 125°C (255°F), whisk the egg whites in a stand mixer on a low–medium speed, until soft peaks form.

When the sugar mixture reaches 130°C (265°F), remove it from the heat. With the mixer still running, carefully pour the sugar mixture into the whisking egg whites. It's best to tip it down the sides of the bowl, not directly onto the whites. Mix for 10 minutes, until fully incorporated, then stop the mixer and change the attachment from a whisk to a paddle. Mix with the paddle for a few minutes on a low speed until the mixture becomes a little matte in appearance. Stir through the melted chocolate with a spatula, scraping the sides of the bowl as you go, to ensure an even mix. Add the warm almonds and stir until just combined.

Working quickly, spoon the nougat into the tray. Flatten and spread it evenly, ensuring that all corners are level. Cover the top with the remaining rice paper, dull side up, then use a small rolling pin to gently smooth over the top. Set aside for at least 8 hours at room temperature, until set. Once set, turn the nougat out onto a chopping board and cut it into desired portions.

Store in a cool dark place for up to 3 months. Do not store it in the fridge, as the humidity will turn the nougat soft and sticky.

Gingerbread

Gingerbread is just wonderful! Deeply spiced with warming black pepper, ginger, cinnamon and cloves, the aromas will fill your home as they bake and transport you back in time. Gingerbread is particularly enchanting for children, who can create endless shapes and decorate to their heart's content. Let go of expectations and spend an afternoon making these with the little people in your life, creating food memories and connections that will last a lifetime. Make it an annual tradition they can look back on with fondness, and remember to take photos.

The flavours in this gingerbread linger for a long time, and the beautiful warming spices leave you wanting more. It also lasts well once baked, making it an ideal gift.

SEASONS ALTERED

We like the spice in this dough just so, but you can alter it to your tastes. Vary the flavour by adding raspberry juice to the icing, adding a pop of colour as you go.

Makes 20 large gingerbread

225 g (8 oz) unsalted butter, roughly chopped, at room temperature

170 g (6 oz) soft brown sugar

30 g (1 oz) honey

160 g (5½ oz) golden syrup (or honey, if golden syrup unavailable)

390 g (14 oz) plain (all-purpose) flour

130 g (4½ oz) rye flour

15 g (½ oz) cocoa powder

10 g (¼ oz) ground ginger

4 g (⅛ oz) ground cloves

5 g (⅛ oz) ground cinnamon

1 teaspoon ground black pepper

¾ teaspoon bicarbonate of soda (baking soda)

1 teaspoon fine sea salt

1 large egg, at room temperature

Icing

1 egg white

250 g (9 oz) icing (confectioners') sugar, sifted

1 teaspoon lemon juice

In a stand mixer fitted with the paddle attachment, cream the butter, sugar, honey and golden syrup for 8–10 minutes on medium speed, until pale and fluffy.

Combine the flours, cocoa powder, spices, bicarbonate of soda and salt in a bowl and mix well.

Lightly beat the egg and add it to the creamed butter mixture. Scrape down the side of the bowl as necessary, and mix until just combined.

Using a spatula, fold the dry ingredients into the butter mixture. Fold until just incorporated, so everything is evenly mixed, while being careful not to overmix. Take the mixture out of the bowl and gently knead on a worktop for a few minutes, then flatten it into a large disc. Wrap and refrigerate for at least 1 hour before use.

Preheat the oven to 170°C (340°F). Line two baking trays with baking paper.

On a lightly floured surface, roll out the gingerbread dough to 5–6 mm (¼ in) thick. Use cookie cutters to cut out your desired shapes and lay them out on your trays. You can reuse the scraps. Bake for 10 minutes, then rotate the tray and bake for another 3–4 minutes, until the edges of the gingerbread are just turning a deeper brown. The longer you bake it, the crisper your gingerbread will be. Set aside to cool on a wire rack.

When you're ready to decorate, make the icing by mixing all the ingredients into a smooth paste. Transfer it into a piping bag fitted with a fine nozzle, and pipe decorations onto your gingerbread. Store in an airtight container for up to a week.

Hot cross buns

Late March into April is a beautiful time of year in Melbourne. The days are still warm, but the sting has gone out of the sun. And although hot cross buns were created for the northern spring, somehow they seem wholly more appropriate as an autumn bake.

Traditionally only baked with a cross on Good Friday, these days the frenzy for hot cross buns starts to build straight after Christmas. We're slowly recovering after baking and serving thousands of them each season. We're even learning to enjoy them again – after all, what's not to like? A wholesome spiced bun, lightly glazed, served warm with lashings of good cultured butter.

There are several factors in making a great bun, starting as always with the ingredients. Use the freshest spices you can for bold flavour, always grating the nutmeg yourself. You need to use strong bakers flour for this dough, so it will hold its structure when mixing. If you can't find mixed peel and don't have time to make it, just use the zest of one lemon and one orange. Your buns will lack the toothsome quality the mixed peel brings, but the flavour will still be good.

You'll need to start a day ahead to soak the fruit; if it isn't soaked, the fruit has a tendency to burn on the crust. If you want to make these over two days, just refrigerate the dough overnight after the first fold and finish off the buns the following day.

SEASONS ALTERED

You can find almost endless varieties of hot cross buns out in the wild, as bakeries try to appeal to the masses. We eschew a chocolate version, but have been known to switch out mixed peel for dried cranberries. Mixed peel can be divisive, and the cranberries provide a little sourness, which works really well.

Makes 12

Dough

260 g (9 oz) full-cream (whole) milk

1 medium orange, unpeeled

500 g (1 lb 2 oz) bakers (strong) flour, plus 50 g (1¾ oz) extra

40 g (1½ oz) soft brown sugar

10 g (¼ oz) fine sea salt

1 medium egg, at room temperature

20 g (¾ oz) fresh yeast or 10 g (¼ oz) dried yeast

50 g (1¾ oz) unsalted butter, softened

80 g (2¾ oz) currants, soaked in water overnight

80 g (2¾ oz) sultanas, soaked in water overnight

80 g (2¾ oz) raisins, soaked in water overnight

6 g (⅕ oz) ground cinnamon

1 g (¹⁄₃₂ oz) ground allspice

3 g (¹⁄₁₀ oz) freshly grated nutmeg

1 g (¹⁄₃₂ oz) ground clove

60 g (2 oz) mixed peel (see page 215)

Brown sugar glaze

100 g (3½ oz) soft brown sugar

100 g (3½ oz) water

1 cinnamon stick

1 star anise

5 cloves

Cross mix

80 g (2¾ oz) plain (all-purpose) flour

pinch of fine sea salt

pinch of caster (superfine) sugar

70 g (2½ oz) water

15 g (½ oz) neutral-flavoured vegetable oil

Egg wash

1 egg

splash of full-cream (whole) milk

pinch of fine sea salt

To make the brown sugar glaze, combine the sugar, water and spices in a small saucepan over a low heat. Bring it to the boil slowly, stirring constantly until the sugar has dissolved, then reduce the heat and simmer gently for about 5 minutes to infuse the spices. The mixture will reduce slightly, making a fragrant, sticky glaze. Pour the glaze into a container and store it at room temperature until required.

To start the bun dough, slowly bring the milk to a simmer in a saucepan over a medium heat, being careful not to let it boil. Remove from the heat and set aside to cool.

Place the orange in a saucepan and cover well with water. Bring to the boil, reduce the heat slightly and continue to boil for about 1 hour, until a knife goes through it easily. Drain, and when cool enough to handle, quarter the orange and remove any pips. Place it in a blender and blend for a minute or two, until you have a smooth purée, then set aside to cool.

Combine 500 g (1 lb 2 oz) of the flour with the sugar and salt in the bowl of a stand mixer fitted with the dough hook, and stir to combine. In a separate bowl, lightly whisk together the milk, egg and yeast, and add to the dry ingredients. Mix for 5 minutes on a medium speed, then stop the mixer and scrape down the side and base of the bowl with a spatula to ensure that all of the dry mix is incorporated and that the mixture is forming one large ball of dough. Mix for another 6–8 minutes until the dough is smooth and strong, and comes away easily from the side of the bowl.

With the mixer still running, incorporate the butter, a little at a time. Make sure it is being incorporated into the dough and not just coating the side of the bowl – you may need to stop and scrape down the sides once or twice. Mix for 2–3 minutes, until the dough is firm and shiny, not sticky or wet. Use the windowpane test to check the dough. Take a small ball of dough and gently stretch it between your hands – you should be able to stretch it very thin without it breaking. If you find that it breaks easily, mix for a few more minutes to continue working the gluten in the flour, then test it again. If you are mixing by hand, this step will take a good 15 minutes of folding.

Once your dough has reached the right consistency, add 70 g (2½ oz) of the orange puree (you can freeze the rest for later use).

Drain the fruit and sprinkle the remaining 50 g (1¾ oz) of flour over it and spices. Add the fruit and the mixed peel to the dough, then mix for 2–3 minutes, until the fruit is evenly dispersed. Be careful not to overmix, to avoid the fruit breaking down.

Turn the dough out onto a lightly floured bench and knead it for about 1 minute, then place it in a lightly greased bowl and fold it by lifting it up and over itself a few times, turning the bowl 90 degrees between each fold. Leave the dough to rest in the bowl, covered with a damp tea towel (dish towel), for 1 hour. If you want to spread the workload over a couple of days, the dough will be fine left in the fridge overnight at this point.

Knead the dough in the bowl for about 1 minute, then fold the dough by lifting it up and over onto itself a few times, turning the bowl 90 degrees between each fold. Leave it to rest, covered with the damp tea towel for up to 1 hour, or until risen by half. Gently press the dough; it's ready if your finger leaves a dent in the surface. If the dough springs back quickly, leave it longer, and then test again.

Turn the dough out onto a lightly floured bench and cut it into twelve equal pieces. Take each piece and gently flatten the dough, then bring the edges together in the middle so it forms a rough ball. Turn it over so the seam is at the bottom, then cup your hand over the dough and roll it on the bench using firm pressure until it forms a nice tight round ball with a smooth, even surface.

Line a baking tray with baking paper. Using firm pressure, roll each ball on the bench again. Putting pressure on the bun strengthens the dough; you want a round, firm ball that sits up on the bench rather than a saggy form.

Place the buns on the lined tray, evenly spaced out to allow for the eventual rise.

Cover with a damp tea towel and leave to rise for 1½–2 hours, until risen by half. Test the buns again by gently pressing the surface – if your finger leaves a dent, you're ready to bake; if the dough springs back it still needs more time.

Preheat the oven to 200°C (390°F). To prepare the cross mix, combine all the ingredients in a bowl and whisk until a smooth paste forms. Put this into a piping (icing) bag with a plain nozzle and set aside.

Make the egg wash by lightly whisking the egg, milk and salt in a small mixing bowl, then brush it evenly over the buns. Pipe a cross onto each bun.

Put the tray in the oven, reduce the temperature to 180°C (360°F) and bake for 10 minutes. Turn the tray and bake for a further 4–6 minutes, until golden brown. While the buns are baking, warm the brown sugar glaze in a small saucepan. Once they are baked, lightly brush the surface of your buns with the syrup. Cool slightly on a wire rack, but not for too long. They are best eaten when still warm, although they're also excellent the next day, toasted and spread with lots of butter.

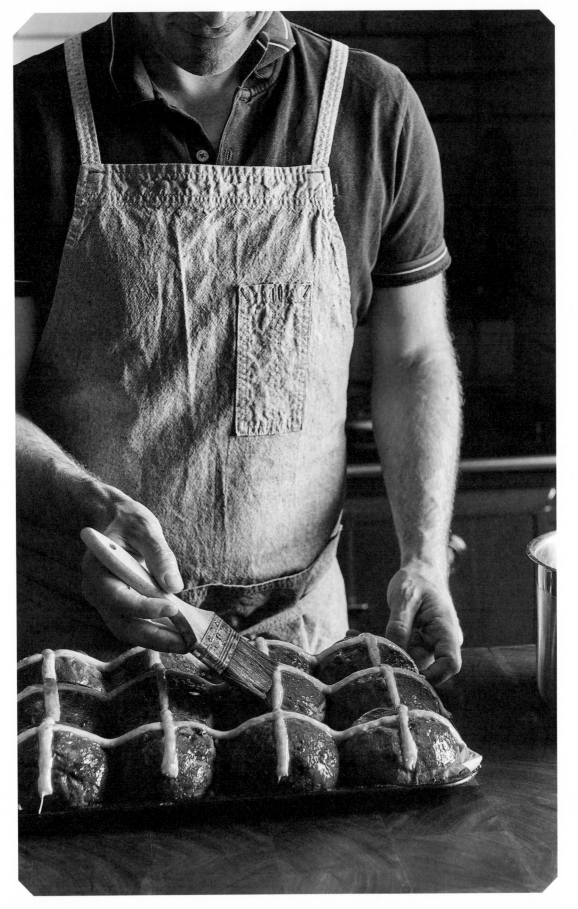

Seasons captured

Preserving the glut for
simple pleasures

Pages 191–217

Our journey of preserving has been like a dive down the rabbit hole. We have many books on jam making, pickling and fermenting, canning and more, and love to spend hours reading and experimenting. We're driven by a fascination with the processes, a quest for deliciousness, a rejection of processed foods and an abhorrence of waste. We often look at the ends of our produce and wonder what can be done with it, determined to use every last scrap. There is something delightfully homestead-y about preserving in all the ways.

Growing up in Cornwall, Michael spent summers walking between hedgerows enjoying the heady scents of elderflower and hawthorn. Central Victoria has pockets of elderflowers that flower early in summer. The perfume is irresistible, almost begging to be captured. Lemon-scented verbena is similarly lovely. The cordials here are a great way to capture the season, to be enjoyed for months afterwards.

We love to use what's around us, and often walk through our neighbourhood looking for inspiration. Our local WhatsApp group, created during the interminable Melbourne COVID-19 lockdowns and still thriving, sees neighbours gifting and swapping homegrown produce, along with hand-me-down toys and clothes. Our suburb was home to many Greek settlers, and fig trees abound. We've been known to pinch the odd fig leaf on a Sunday afternoon stroll to make a fragrant custard, perfect for a simple dessert to close out the weekend.

Homemade jam can't be beaten. Here we have a jam of berries, one of stone fruit and, of course, a citrus marmalade. Take these recipes and make them your own, depending on the season and what's in abundance. Enjoy your jam knowing there are no nasties preserving it and eat with your senses – the smell of real fruit, the vibrant colour and the full flavour make it so much better than mass-produced, shop-bought jam. The berry compote is like a fresh jam, a quick way to use up fruit before you lose it.

Pippa's mother has a prolific garden of citrus trees, endlessly useful in preserving. Lemon curd makes a bright and useful addition to your larder. Lemonade, marmalade, mixed peel and candied cumquats extend their usefulness even further.

The best thing about many of these recipes is their versatility. Apple sauce, for example, is pure comfort in a jar, and can be served alongside roast pork or a little cheese, used to top a bowl of yoghurt, to add sweetness to smoothies or baked into muffins. The recipes themselves are endlessly adaptable. Once you've familiarised yourself with the techniques, you're ready to have fun with them.

It's easy to lean into the romance of these old traditions, but there is also sense in them. Take fruit in full glut – perfectly ripe, locally grown and free or inexpensive. You can't possibly eat it all, and it would be a crime to throw it out. Using sugar or salt, time and technique, you can transform the most basic of ingredients into something to be enjoyed for months, improving all the while. As our climate heats and geopolitical tensions increase the world over, we can take comfort from a well-stocked larder. Knowing there's a small treat ready for when you need it is like money in the bank.

Verbena lemonade

Years ago, when we were first setting up Tivoli Road Bakery, we took the decision not to buy in bottled water or soft drinks. We couldn't abide the bottling and selling of a product that was freely available and essential to life, nor the excessive use of glass, or the rubbish ingredients and insane amounts of sugar that go into most packaged fizzy drinks. We installed a water carbonating unit, and then decided it would be unethical to charge for water, sparkling or still. In order to break even on the cost of the unit, we set about creating soda syrups so we could value-add.

Lemon-scented verbena is a beautifully aromatic perennial herb that's worth growing just to experience the perfume in your garden on a summer's evening. It makes a soothing after-dinner tisane, and is fantastic infused into the milk used to make custard or yoghurt. This lemonade is not too sweet and wonderfully refreshing.

SEASONS ALTERED

Use your favourite herb to alter this recipe, or a mixture. Lemon thyme or fresh bay leaves are wonderful. Adjust the sugar to your taste.

Makes 800 g (1 lb 12 oz)

30 g (1 oz) fresh verbena

300 g (10½ oz) boiled water

250 g (9 oz) lemon juice

300 g (10½ oz) caster
    (superfine) sugar

Steep the verbena in the boiled water for at least 1 hour, or until cool. Strain the leaves, reserving the liquid.

Combine the verbena infusion, lemon juice and sugar in a saucepan and bring to a simmer over a medium heat, stirring to dissolve the sugar. Once the sugar has dissolved, remove the saucepan from the heat. Store the syrup in sterilised bottles (page 17) for a year or more. Refrigerate and use within 2 weeks after opening.

Dilute to taste with sparkling water and serve over ice, garnished with a couple of fresh verbena leaves. A good slug of gin is optional and delightful.

Elderflower cordial

The scent of elderflower is intoxicating, evoking memories of summers past while bringing joy to the present season. We've discovered a few pockets of elderflower, not far from Melbourne, some more secret than others. It's definitely worth a detour to gather and capture the delicious fragrance, and then literally bottle it.

SEASONS ALTERED

Elderflower is a particularly special thing, one that we seek to find and don't seek to alter. There would be other plants you could use, but in all honesty we haven't found anything better.

Raw sugar creates a richly hued syrup. You could use caster sugar if you prefer a paler cordial.

Makes approximately 2 litres (68 fl oz)

20–30 heads elderflower
grated zest of 2 lemons
1–2 litres (34–68 fl oz) water
1.5 kg (3 lb 5 oz) raw
    (demerara) sugar
300 g (10½ oz) lemon juice

Use scissors to cut your elderflower heads from their stems. Place all the cut heads into a large bowl with the lemon zest.

Fill and boil your kettle, and pour enough boiled water into the bowl to cover the elderflower. You want it fully submerged but still densely packed, not wallowing in water. Cover the bowl with a clean tea towel (dish towel) and leave to steep for at least 6 hours, or overnight.

Strain the liquid through a fine muslin cloth and squeeze the elderflower heads to extract all the juice. Weigh the elderflower-infused liquid and transfer to a large saucepan.

For every 500 g (1 lb 2 oz) of liquid, use 350 g (12½ oz) sugar and 50 g (1¾ oz) of lemon juice. Add the sugar and lemon juice to the saucepan and place it over a medium–high heat. Bring it to a simmer, stirring to dissolve the sugar, then set aside to cool. Once cool, strain once more into a jug, then pour into sterilised bottles (page 17) and seal immediately. You can also freeze the cordial in ice cube trays for later use.

Dilute to taste (a ratio of 1 part cordial to 6 parts water works well) and serve over ice for a refreshing drink, or use elderflower cordial to make Summer pudding (page 172).

Berry and rose geranium compote

A quick and easy way to make your fruit go further, a compote is a great way to use up those berries you bought excitedly at the market but didn't finish when they were at their peak. While the leaves of rose geranium are not edible, they can be used to infuse any number of things with a gentle, rose-like scent – just be sure to remove them before you eat the compote.

Enjoy your compote warm or cold, over porridge, pancakes, cake, Greek yoghurt or ice cream, or fold it through freshly whipped cream to fill your sponge. Endlessly adaptable and infinitely useful.

SEASONS ALTERED

You're only really limited by your imagination in the making of this cheat's jam. Any mix of berries work here, and you can even add some apple or rhubarb into the mix. Try strawberry gum, lemon myrtle, cinnamon myrtle or fresh bay leaves in place of rose geranium.

Makes 200 g (7 oz)

300 g (10½ oz) mixed berries
60 g (2 oz) raw caster (superfine) sugar
15 g (½ oz) lemon juice
4–5 rose geranium leaves

Hull the berries and rinse them under cold water. Put them in a saucepan with the sugar, lemon juice and rose geranium leaves. Place the pan over a low–medium heat and bring it to a gentle simmer, stirring to dissolve the sugar and mix everything together. Continue to cook, stirring occasionally, for 15–20 minutes, until the berries soften and start to release their juices and the compote thickens.

Remove from the heat and serve immediately or allow to cool. Store in an airtight container in the fridge for up to 1 week.

Strawberry and lemon verbena jam

We have had a potted tree of lemon-scented verbena for many years. Every spring it bursts back to life after looking half dead all winter, filling the garden with its delicious perfume. It is a thirsty plant, but otherwise easy to maintain, and nothing compares to the intense fragrance of the freshly picked leaves. Over the years we've learned different ways to use it, and jamming it with spring's first strawberries is one of the best.

Strawberries are low in pectin, which you need to set your jam. Jam sugar contains pectin, so is useful for achieving the perfect set. Alternatively, you could add pectin powder, available from most supermarkets, or grate an apple into a muslin bag and add this to the saucepan with the fruit. Pectin is naturally occurring; we use an apple pectin made of powdered dehydrated apple skins.

Making jam is one of the most basic preserving methods, and a decidedly useful skill to have. Get yourself a good thermometer and learn the plate test, and summer will be forever at your fingertips. If you are making jam for gifting or storing, be sure to sterilise your jars meticulously (page 18).

SEASONS ALTERED

Strawberries, in particular, lend themselves to herbal infusions. Use lemon thyme in place of verbena, or elderflower if you can find a good local source. Serve on toast or over rice pudding, and enjoy the fruits of summer all year round.

Makes 1.2 litres (41 fl oz)

1 kg (2 lb 3 oz) strawberries
800 g (1 lb 12 oz) jam sugar
70 g (2½ oz) lemon juice
2 sprigs lemon verbena, leaves
    picked and roughly chopped
grated zest of 1 lemon

Wash, dry and hull the strawberries. Put them in a large bowl or container with the sugar and toss to coat. Refrigerate overnight, and place a small plate into the freezer for later.

The next day, combine the macerated strawberries with the lemon juice in a large saucepan over low heat. Slowly simmer for a few minutes, until the berries start to break down, stirring to completely dissolve the sugar.

Once the sugar is fully dissolved, turn up the heat and boil the mixture rapidly for 15–20 minutes, stirring frequently so it doesn't stick on the bottom of the pan. As it boils, a light foam will form on the surface; just skim this off with a spoon as it appears.

Use a thermometer to monitor your jam, and as soon as it reaches 104°C (220°F), turn off the heat and use the plate test to check the consistency. Add the chopped lemon verbena leaves and lemon zest, and set aside to cool and infuse for 10 minutes, stirring from time to time to keep the fruit from dropping to the bottom. Pour the jam into hot sterilised jars and seal immediately.

The bright acidity and vibrant colour of raspberries make this a great favourite, and infusing the jam with lemon thyme adds an alluring layer. This is our favourite jam to enjoy with toast or a plain croissant, and is also great at the base of a fruit galette. It is used in the Bakewell tart (page 142) and the Pistachio and raspberry wagon wheel (page 118).

SEASONS ALTERED

Use the recipe as a guide and use whatever berries you have to hand. Blackberries, boysenberries, mulberries, blueberries, strawberries, or any combination of them, are wonderful. You may choose to omit the lemon thyme for a simpler berry jam.

Makes 1.2 litres (41 fl oz)

700 g (1 lb 9 oz) jam sugar
1 kg (2 lb 3 oz) raspberries, rinsed
70 g (2½ oz) lemon juice
1 tablespoon lemon thyme leaves
grated zest of 1 lemon

Preheat the oven to 110°C (230°F). Put the sugar in a large, clean baking dish and warm it in the oven while you prepare your fruit. Put a small plate in the freezer for later.

Combine the raspberries and lemon juice in a saucepan over a low heat. Slowly stew them for a couple of minutes, until the berries start to break down a little.

Add the warm sugar in four batches, stirring to completely dissolve each addition before adding the next. Once the sugar is fully incorporated, turn up the heat and boil the mixture rapidly for 10–15 minutes, stirring frequently so it doesn't stick on the bottom of the pan. As it boils, a light foam will form on the surface; just skim this off with a spoon as it appears.

Use a thermometer to monitor your jam, and as soon as it reaches 104°C (220°F) turn off the heat and use the plate test (see details opposite) to check the consistency. Add the lemon thyme and lemon zest, and set aside to cool and infuse for 10 minutes, stirring from time to time to keep the fruit from dropping to the bottom. Pour the jam into hot sterilised jars and seal immediately.

Apricot and amaretto jam

Apricot jam is so versatile and the colour is spectacular. We use it often in some of our favourite bakes, such as Bakewell tart (page 144), Cream cheese rugelach (page 134), or heated to form a light glaze for a simple cake or tart. Apricot is the first stone fruit to appear in the summer, and we always aim to preserve some in various ways, to hold onto the feeling of promise that the warmer months bring.

Keep the kernels of your apricots when preparing them. Wrap them in muslin with the lemon pips and zest, and add them to your saucepan. They'll add an almond-like flavour and release pectin as your jam heats.

SEASONS ALTERED

Amaretto is a liqueur made from apricot kernels, sometimes mixed with bitter almonds. Apricot kernels contain traces of arsenic, so are toxic eaten in large quantities, but the bitter almond flavour they impart through infusion is wonderful. Apricots and almonds are related, making them an ideal flavour match. Frangelico or Drambuie are both great alternatives in this jam.

Makes 1 litre (2 kg 3 oz)

700 g (1 lb 9 oz) raw
 (demerara) sugar
1 kg (2 lb 3 oz) apricots
grated zest and pips of 1 lemon
70 g (2½ oz) lemon juice
100 g (3½ oz) water
80 g (2¾ oz) amaretto

Preheat the oven to 110°C (230°F). Put the sugar in a large, clean baking dish and warm it in the oven while you prepare your fruit. Put a small plate in the freezer for later.

De-stone the apricots, cut them into eighths and put them in a large saucepan. Use a vegetable peeler to peel the zest off the lemons, and then juice them, reserving the pips. Wrap the apricot kernels, lemon pips and strips of lemon zest in muslin and add it to the saucepan. Add the lemon juice and water, and give it all a stir with a wooden spoon.

Place the saucepan over a medium heat and bring it to a simmer. Simmer for around 10 minutes, until the apricots have softened and the mixture thickens a little.

Reduce the heat to low and add the warm sugar, stirring for a few minutes to dissolve it. Once the sugar is dissolved, turn the heat up and boil your jam for around 20 minutes, stirring frequently to prevent it from sticking to the bottom of the pan.

Use a thermometer to monitor your jam, and as soon as it reaches 104°C (220°F) turn off the heat and use the plate test (page 18) to check the consistency. Add the amaretto, remove the muslin bag, squeezing all the juices back into the pan. Give your jam a good stir, then carefully ladle into hot sterilised jars and seal immediately.

Seville orange marmalade

Seville oranges are bitter to eat and therefore destined to become marmalade. We make an annual batch during their short season so we have it on hand to eat on toast or crumpets, or to make Zucchini and marmalade muffins (page 76).

SEASONS ALTERED

Feel free to use grapefruit, lemon, lime or a mixture. Make a large batch to last a year and give some to your marmalade-loving friends.

Makes 1.5 litres (3 lb 5 oz)

450 g (1 lb) unwaxed Seville oranges
1125 g (6 lb 3½ oz) water
70 g (2½ oz) lemon juice
900 g (2 lb) caster (superfine) sugar

Make thin incisions to mark quarters in the oranges, then peel off the rind in petals, leaving the orange intact with the pith still attached. Slice the rind into thin strips and set aside.

Cut the oranges in half and put them in a blender. Blend until pureed, then strain the juice through a sieve into a saucepan, pressing the pulp into the sieve to extract as much juice as possible. Tie the remaining pulp, pith and seeds in a muslin cloth and add to the saucepan. Add the water and lemon juice, together with the strips of rind.

Bring the mixture to a simmer over a medium heat. Simmer for 1 hour, until the rind softens completely. Remove the muslin bag and squeeze it tightly, pouring the juice back into the saucepan.

Gradually add the sugar in three batches, stirring until each addition has dissolved before adding the next.

Once the sugar is fully incorporated, turn up the heat and boil the mixture rapidly for 10–15 minutes, stirring frequently so it doesn't stick on the bottom of the pan. As it boils, a light foam will form on the surface; just skim this off with a spoon as it appears.

Use a thermometer to monitor your marmalade, and as soon as it reaches 104°C (220°F) turn off the heat and use the plate test (page 18) to check the consistency. Set aside to cool for 10 minutes, stirring from time to time to keep the fruit from dropping to the bottom. Pour into hot sterilised jars and seal immediately.

Lemon curd makes a lovely gift of your bounty, a yellow little jar of sunshine. It's zingy and sweet, and delicious on soft fresh bread or toasted crumpets.

Makes 350 g (12½ oz)

95 g (3¼ oz) caster
   (superfine) sugar

4 egg yolks

90 g (3 oz) lemon juice

95 g (3¼ oz) unsalted butter,
   cut into cubes and softened

In a large mixing bowl, whisk together the sugar and egg yolks, then whisk in the lemon juice. Place the bowl over a pan filled halfway with water (ensuring the bowl doesn't touch the water). Place it over a low heat for about 25 minutes, stirring regularly until it reaches 80°C (175°F) on a sugar thermometer, and becomes thick. You don't want the mixture to boil, just to stay warm so it thickens and all the ingredients are cooked.

Once you have a thick consistency, gradually add the cubes of softened butter and whisk to emulsify.

Cool in the fridge for 2–3 hours before using. Refrigerate for up to 1 week, or store at room temperature in sterilised jars (page 17) for several months.

Poached quinces

Quinces have the most wonderful perfume. When quinces are cooked low and slow, their intoxicating aromas are released, filling the home. Eat these simply with a little cream or yoghurt or topped with granola, or pull out all the stops and make the Quince and hazelnut sherry trifle (page 170).

As with all slow and tedious kitchen jobs, preparing quinces is a task best shared. Boil the kettle, put on some music and enjoy a chat as you go. It's good communal cooking, and makes the time go by faster. They're also best enjoyed in community – gifted in jars or made up into an impressive dessert.

SEASONS ALTERED

The poaching liquid can also be reduced to create a syrup that you can drizzle over the quince or use to make cocktails.

We also love to vary the spices. Cardamom pods, whole cloves, whole star anise, fresh bay leaves and whole allspice all work well.

Makes 700 g (1 lb 9 oz)

800 g (1 lb 12 oz) raw
   (demerara) sugar
1 kg (2 lb 3 oz) water
2–3 cinnamon quills
grated zest and juice of 1 orange
grated zest and juice of 1 lemon
1 kg (2 lb 3 oz) quinces

Preheat the oven to 120°C (250°F).

Place the sugar and water in a wide ovenproof pan –a large cast-iron casserole dish is ideal – and bring to a simmer over a high heat. Add the cinnamon, juice and zests and return to the simmer.

Peel the quinces and cut them into quarters, removing the cores. Wrap the peel, cores and pips in muslin and add to the syrup. Place the quince pieces into the syrup as you go to prevent discolouration. Cover the surface with a cartouche: take a piece of baking paper and fold it in half, then fold it in half again to make a small square. Fold it again to make a triangle, with the loose edges of the paper at the top. Continue like this until you have a narrow wedge shape. Hold it over your pan with the point at the centre, snip the loose edges at the radius and unfold to reveal a round of baking paper that neatly covers the surface of your pan.

Return the syrup to a simmer, then cover with a lid and place your pan in the oven until your quince reaches the desired tenderness and colour: 4–5 hours will give you a medium ruby red; 6–7 hours creates a deep burgundy. For a very deep colour, turn off the oven after 7 hours and leave in the oven overnight to cool completely.

Once ready, sterilise your jars (page 17) and fill them with quince. Pour the syrup over the top to cover completely and seal immediately. They will keep for months at room temperature. Refrigerate after opening.

Fig leaf custard

The flavour of cream infused with fig leaves is a bit of a revelation, with amazingly fresh, floral notes. Fig trees proliferate in the alleyways of our neighbourhood, where you will often find us loitering with a bag, collecting the leaves.

Take a blind-baked tart shell, fill it with fig leaf custard and top with fresh blackberries for a delicious summer dessert. This custard can also be used to fill doughnuts or other pastries, or just enjoyed in a bowl with fresh fruit.

SEASONS ALTERED

There's a whole world of custard beyond vanilla. Use raspberry leaf, lemon-scented verbena or fresh bay leaves and enjoy the variety of flavours you can achieve.

Makes 500 g (1 lb 2 oz)

4–5 whole fig leaves

500 g (1 lb 2 oz) full-cream (whole) milk

6 egg yolks

60 g (2 oz) caster (superfine) sugar

40 g (1½ oz) plain (all-purpose) flour

Wash the fig leaves and trim any woody stems. Take care not to cut into the leaf, as this will release a white liquid which will spoil the flavour of your custard and can irritate the skin. Place the leaves into a large bowl. Put the milk in a saucepan and bring it up to a simmer over a medium heat. Pour the warm milk over the fig leaves and set aside to infuse for up to 1 hour.

Strain the milk and return it to the pan, discarding the fig leaves. Place the pan over a medium heat, and while the milk is returning to a simmer, whisk together the egg yolks and sugar until slightly pale. Add the flour and whisk to combine.

Pour the milk over the egg mixture, whisking constantly as you go to avoid scrambling the eggs.

Return the custard to the saucepan and cook over a low heat for around 5 minutes, stirring constantly to avoid burning. Alternate between using a whisk and a spatula – the whisk helps to thoroughly mix everything and get rid of any lumps as they appear; the spatula can be used to scrape the sides and base of the saucepan to stop any spots catching as the custard cooks. This results in a smooth, consistent custard with no risk of scorching. The custard will become thick, and just start to bubble. As soon as this happens, remove it from the heat and strain the custard through a fine sieve into a clean bowl.

Lay a piece of baking paper over the surface to avoid a skin forming, and refrigerate the custard to cool it completely. Refrigerate for up to 5 days.

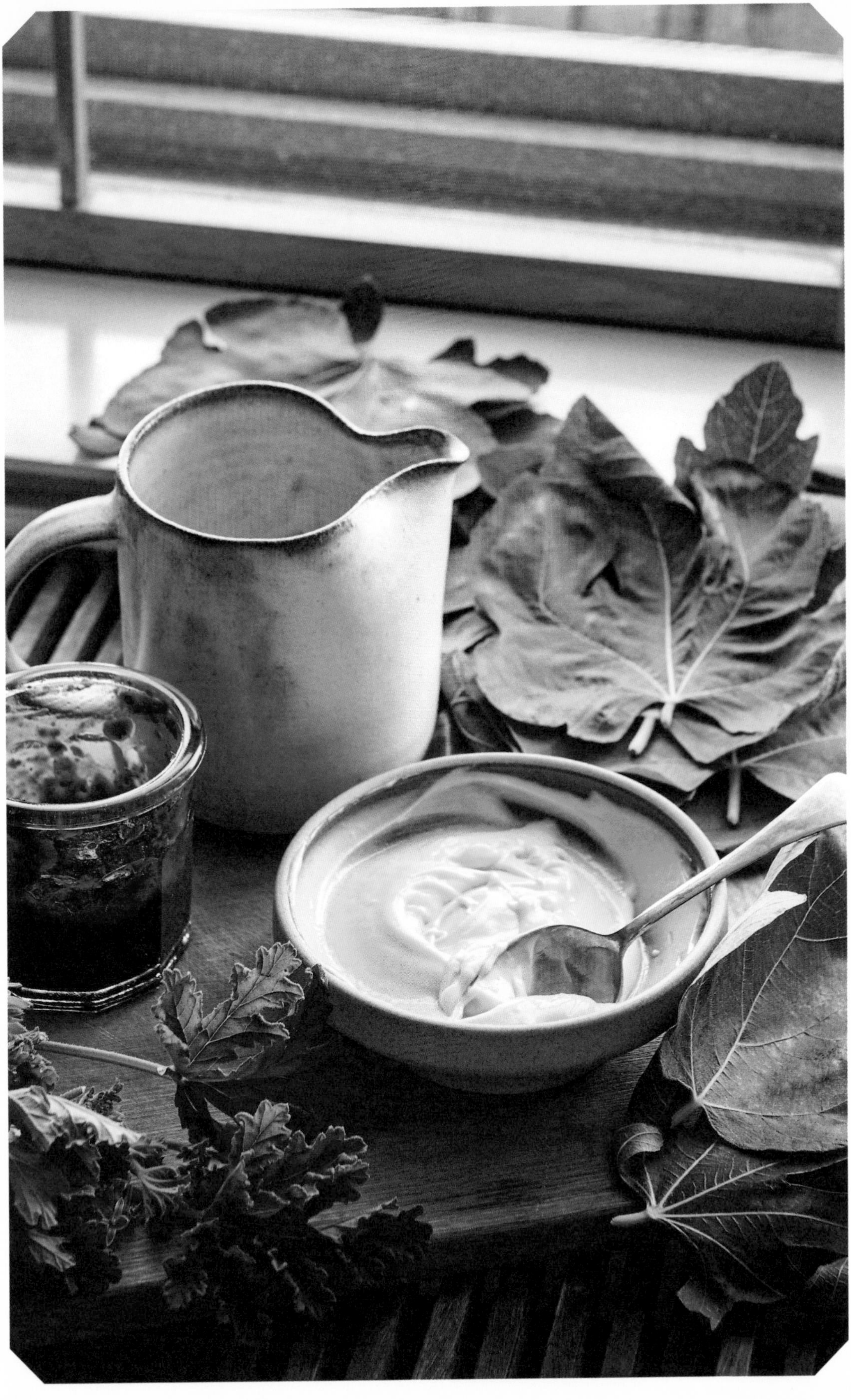

Apple sauce

Apple sauce is a great way to preserve an abundance of fruit and has many uses, both sweet and savoury. Delicious with roasted pork, we use it to top desserts, add sweetness to smoothies and muffins, over pancakes or waffles, or simply swirl it through thick plain yoghurt.

SEASONS SAVOURED

If you're lucky enough to have access to a diverse orchard, pick your favourite variety of apple or use a medley. Different varieties ripen at different times, so our general recommendation is to use whatever is in season and good for cooking – Granny Smith, Pippin, Gravenstein, McIntosh, Fuji and Jonathan are all great options.

If you're making apple sauce for the purposes of savoury eating, omit the ground spices or replace them with mint leaves and remove them before jarring.

Makes 800 g (1 lb 12 oz)

8–10 apples, approximately 1.2 kg
  (2 lb 10 oz)
grated zest and juice of 1 lemon
½ teaspoon ground cinnamon
¼ teaspoon ground ginger
150 g (5½ oz) water
½ teaspoon fine sea salt
100 g (3½ oz) raw caster
  (superfine) sugar

Peel, core and quarter your apples, and put them in a large saucepan. Add the lemon zest and juice, cinnamon, ginger, water and salt. Add half the sugar, reserving the rest to add to taste later on.

Place the saucepan over a high heat and bring the mixture to the boil. Reduce the heat to low and simmer gently for 15–20 minutes, until the apples are cooked through and completely soft. For a chunky apple sauce, break up the cooked apples with a spoon. Alternatively, transfer them to a food processor and blitz to your desired consistency. Pour the hot sauce into hot sterilised jars or bottles (page 17) and seal immediately. The apple sauce will keep for many months stored in the pantry. Refrigerate after opening and use within 2 weeks.

It can be hard to find good mixed peel in the shops, and making your own is a great way to use up the peel of any citrus fruit. Waste not, want not. A large batch will see you through the year, for Christmas mince pies (page 172) and Hot cross buns (page 186). You will taste the difference if you use good quality fruit. Always seek out unwaxed citrus when using the peel or zest.

There are many traditional bakes that make use of this divisive ingredient (like coriander, some people love it and others hate it with a passion). If you're firmly in team mixed peel and an adventurous baker, have a go at making Panettone or Stollen.

SEASONS ALTERED

When making mixed peel for your seasonal bakes, use a mixture of citrus fruits according to your tastes and availability, such as varieties of orange, lime, lemon, bergamot and grapefruit. Larger strips of candied orange peel make a wonderful after-dinner sweet, served alongside black coffee. You could also dip strips of candied peel into melted dark chocolate. Yum!

**Makes approximately
300 g (10½ oz)**

5 medium-sized citrus fruits
1 kg (2 lb 3 oz) raw caster
   (superfine) sugar

Slice each piece of fruit into eight wedges, then slice the flesh out of each wedge to leave the peel with a little pith still on. Set aside the flesh for juice or a snack, and slice the peel into 4–5 mm (¼ in) wide strips. Put the peel in a heavy-based saucepan pan, cover well with cold water and place over a high heat. Bring to the boil and then reduce the heat to simmer for 5 minutes.

Drain the peel and return it to the pan. Cover again with cold water, bring to the boil, then reduce the heat to simmer for 20 minutes. Drain the liquid, reserving the water this time.

Preheat the oven to its lowest temperature (about 60°C/140°F). Return the reserved water to the saucepan, making a note of its weight. Add an equal weight of sugar to the pan, reserving the remaining sugar, and place it over a medium heat. As a guide, 400 g (14 oz) water and 400 g (14 oz) sugar will generally be enough. Bring the mixture to the boil, stirring constantly until the sugar has dissolved.

Add the peel back to the pan and reduce to a simmer for another 30 minutes, until the peel has softened and turned translucent. Leave the peel to cool slightly in the liquid for about 10 minutes.

Line a tray with baking paper and use a large slotted spoon to transfer the peel onto the tray. Discard the sugar syrup or reserve it for another use. Spread the peel evenly over the tray in a single layer and bake for 30–40 minutes to remove any excess moisture. The texture of the peel will be quite leathery at this stage.

As an option, at this point you could make crystallised peel for snacking on. To do this, place the remaining sugar in a bowl. Add the candied peel a few pieces at a time, and gently toss the peel in the sugar until completely coated. Put the peel back on the tray, evenly spread in a single layer, and leave to dry at room temperature for several hours, preferably overnight.

Candied cumquats

Cumquats seem to be one of those trees that many people have because they're easy to grow and evergreen. The blossom is sweet, and the fruits are like little orange jewels. The tiny fruits are excessively sour and not enjoyable to eat raw, and as a result we see many a cumquat tree surrounded by fallen fruit in our neighbourhood. Better to harvest and harness when you can.

If you are candying your cumquats for gifting or storing, be sure to sterilise your jars meticulously (see page 17). Use in Christmas pudding, or even your hot cross buns.

SEASONS ALTERED

You can use this method to candy other fruit, such as quince, cherries, sour cherries, or even sliced pineapple. Just use the same weight of fruit, and adjust the spices to your taste.

Makes 500 g (1 lb 2 oz)

500 g (1 lb 2 oz) water
400 g (14 oz) raw caster (superfine) sugar
2 cloves
2 star anise
1 vanilla bean, seeds scraped (or 1 teaspoon vanilla paste)
juice of 1 lemon
500 g (1 lb 2 oz) cumquats

Combine the water, sugar, spices and lemon juice in a heavy-based saucepan. Place over a medium heat and bring to a simmer, stirring constantly until the sugar has dissolved.

Add the cumquats and bring the mixture to the boil, then reduce the heat and simmer for 20–30 minutes, until the fruit is translucent.

Remove from the heat and set aside to cool completely. Spoon the cumquats into hot sterilised jars, and pour the syrup over to cover. Seal the jars immediately and store at room temperature for up to 1 year. Refrigerate after opening.

To the team at Hardie Grant, especially Simon Davis, thank you for picking up *Sweet Seasons* and keeping us on track. Thanks to Kristin Thomas and Murray Batten for the beautiful design, and to Vanessa Lanaway for refining and correcting text with kindness and patience.

To Helen Goh, thank you for your inspiration, enthusiasm and encouragement over the years. And, of course, for your beautiful foreword. You recognised the intent behind our work and brought it to life through your words. A true kindred spirit.

Thanks to Kirsten Jenkins for saying yes! It was a dream to work with you. Your energy, enthusiasm, organisation and brilliance with food made shooting so fun. We'll never look at a trifle the same again!

To Rochelle Eagle, your incredible eye, flexibility, lighting genius and hard work is very much appreciated. You were the quiet, stable presence in the room. You are an artist and together with Kirsten, a dream team indeed.

Ella Cooper, that's three books we've been lucky enough to work on with you. As always your talent, energy and attention to detail was amazing. Thank you for picking up mistakes in the recipes and beautiful results every time. Also: best shoot DJ ever!

Thanks to Ronnen Goren and Trace Streeter for letting us take over your incredible home, and for being so kind and helpful. The Daylesford Longhouse was a dream location.

Many friends supplied amazing produce for testing and shooting the recipes. Thanks to Charlie and Harry at Hunted & Gathered for the best local chocolate, Zac Burd at Burd Eggs for the good eggs, Mancel and Matt at St David Dairy for the mountains of butter and cream, Jo Corrigan and Matthew Donnelly from Force of Nature for incredible strawberries, elderflower, quinces and even a bunch of roses! Thanks to Courtney Young and Ian Congdon from Woodstock Flour for your wonderful fresh wholegrain flour. And to Melbourne Farmers Markets for supporting the many stallholders we are so lucky to buy from every week, in every season.

Thanks to Justine Katjar for recipe testing, lending equipment, and for the Florentine recipe. Thanks to Maaryasha Werdinger for supporting recipe development at Zelda.

To Suzanne Farrel: you have given us preserves, looked after Monty and offered deep, affectionate friendship to our whole family. Thank you.

Thanks to our Cornish family, in particular Paul Jewell and Martha Noall, for recipes, stories and endless chats over cups of tea.

Thanks to Geoff Smith for all the Clover sitting and Monty minding, for being our guinea pig and testing recipes. To Tina Smith, thank you for your support with Clover, being a listening ear and many years of food inspiration and education. Thanks to you both for the very best foundations in food and life.

To our beautiful and wonderful daughter Clover, thank you for being so helpful and patient as this book came together. We love you so so so so so so so so so so much. x

Further reading

We love to read about and discuss all aspects of food. Here are some of the baking books we return to for inspiration and excellent pointers on technique.

Tartine by Elisabeth Pruiett and Chad Robertson
Flour and Stone by Nadine Ingram
Short and Sweet by Dan Lepard
Advanced Bread and Pastry by Michel Suas
Sweet by Yotam Ottolenghi and Helen Goh
Bread, Cake, Doughnuts by Justin Gellatly
Beatrix Bakes by Natalie Paull
Bourke Street Bakery by Paul Allam and David Mcguinness

If you want to dig a little deeper into the power of your food choices to make a difference in the world, recent reads we've loved include *Soil* by Matthew Evans; *Eating to Extinction – The World's Rarest Foods and Why We Need to Save Them* by Dan Saladino, *Why You Should Give a F*ck About Farming* by Gabrielle Chan and *Call of the Reed Warbler – A New Agriculture, A New Earth* by Charles Massey. Organisations such as Australian Food Sovereignty Alliance, GrAiNZ and A Growing Culture offer information and inspiration.

About the authors

Pippa and Michael live in Melbourne with their daughter, Clover. They believe that food has the power to connect us with people, place and planet. They are passionate about regenerative living and dedicated to building abundant and resilient local food systems through their personal and professional lives.

Michael grew up in Penzance, Cornwall, before moving to London, where he met his Australian wife, Pippa. Together they lived in London, Edinburgh and Sydney, before settling in Melbourne in 2008. They opened Tivoli Road Bakery in 2013, dedicated to supporting local farmers and offering high-quality bakes to their community. After garnering a loyal following for their bakery in Melbourne and beyond, Michael and Pippa sold the business to focus on new opportunities.

Their acclaimed first book, *The Tivoli Road Baker*, was published in 2017. Their follow-up book of savoury bakes, *All Day Baking: Savoury, Not Sweet*, was published in 2021. It was selected for the Jamie Oliver Cookbook Club book of the month in May 2022. As co-founders of GrAiNZ, Michael and Pippa are committed to building a healthy and thriving local grain economy. Their new venture, Urbanstead, exists to create a more just and sustainable food system through education and community building.

Published in 2024 by Hardie Grant Books, an imprint of Hardie Grant Publishing

Hardie Grant Books (Melbourne)
Wurundjeri Country
Building 1, 658 Church Street
Richmond, Victoria 3121

Hardie Grant North America
2912 Telegraph Ave
Berkeley, California 94705

hardiegrant.com/books

Hardie Grant acknowledges the Traditional Owners of the Country on which we work,
the Wurundjeri People of the Kulin Nation and the Gadigal People of the Eora Nation,
and recognises their continuing connection to the land, waters and culture.
We pay our respects to their Elders past and present.

A catalogue record for this
book is available from the
National Library of Australia

A catalogue record for this book is available
from the National Library of Australia

Sweet Seasons
ISBN 978 1 74379 944 4
ISBN 978 1 76144 139 4 (ebook)

10 9 8 7 6 5 4 3 2 1

Publisher: Simon Davis
Project Editors: Loran McDougall and Jasmin Chua
Editor: Vanessa Lanaway
Design Manager: Kristin Thomas
Designer: Murray Batten
Photographer: Rochelle Eagle
Stylist: Kirsten Jenkins
Home Economist: Ella Cooper
Head of Production: Todd Rechner
Production Controller: Jessica Harvie

Colour reproduction by Splitting Image Colour Studio
Printed in China by Leo Paper Products LTD.

'What a brilliant book! The moment I started reading it, I wanted to rush into the kitchen and start baking the cakes and pastries that speak to me of love, fun and happiness. Filled with gorgeous cakes and slices that form part of Michael's and Pippa's repertoire from seasons past and present, my favourite (and there are many!) is the cardamom bun. I predict this book will be on the hot list this year!'

Tony Tan

—

'This book proves that for every season and reason in life, a perfect pastry exists to complete the moment. Who better than Michael and Pippa to show you the way.'

Melissa Leong

—

'Pippa and Michael have given us something both inspiring and nostalgic. Full of beautiful recipes, that are delightfully transportive. I feel I've cooked everything in this book without even turning the oven on! A book for bakers, preservers, beginners and dreamers alike. A journey through the seasons that offers a timely reminder that not all preservation happens in a jar.'

Sharon Flynn